Participation Training
for
Adult Education

Participation
Training

FOR ADULT EDUCATION

by Paul Bergevin and John McKinley

THE BETHANY PRESS · ST. LOUIS, MISSOURI

Distributed by Thomas C. Lothian, Melbourne,
Australia, and Auckland, New Zealand and by
The G. R. Welch Company, Toronto, Canada

MANUFACTURED IN THE UNITED STATES OF AMERICA

Introduction

THE PURPOSE OF THIS BOOK is to describe a program of learning which develops a favorable climate for learning through coming to understand one's relationship and responsibility to other persons in the learning process.

By assuming one's responsibilities to others, necessary for participating successfully in this program, an individual can learn to make better use of his own talents and grow toward the kind of free and creative person he has the potential to become.

This book describes a practical idea of adult learning called group-participation training. This program of training in group participation rests upon two assumptions. Both of these assumptions have been verified through experience:

1. that adult learners should have the freedom to assert their individuality
2. that adult learners can learn how to work and learn together cooperatively without injuring the dignity and respect due fellow learners

This manual presents an approach to discussion training that has been used successfully, and is intended as a guide and resource for both trainers and the other participants in the group. Chapters 1, 2, 3, and 5 should be useful for everyone concerned. Chapter 5, however, will be most useful as a resource for all participants after a few sessions have been conducted. Chapter 4 is intended mainly for the trainer, although sections of it are appropriate for all participants.

It must be stated at the outset that persons intending to serve in the role of trainer should have prior experience as a discussion leader and a group participant in a participation-training group. There is no substitute for experience. It is further recommended that beginning trainers (a) work as cotrainer with someone who is experienced in that role if such a person is available, and/or (b) attend a training institute designed to help persons learn how to serve in the role of trainer. Several such institutes in adult education are conducted each year at Indiana University in Bloomington, Indiana, and in many other locations in the United States.

The authors are grateful for the helpful suggestions and editorial assistance given to them by Professor Helen Duncan, Indiana University.

P. B.

J. M.

Table of Contents

7

8

Chapter 1

Participation Training

*Preliminary Questions
and Organization*

A. *What is the purpose of participation training?*

Participation training can be described as an educational means for helping persons help themselves; that is, helping them learn how to learn. This educational program is designed to help the participants accept personal responsibility for self and others in a small-group learning experience. They learn how to learn by participating in a series of learning experiences, by examining their participation as they proceed, and by helping to improve the learning situation.

B. *What does this training accomplish?*

1. Members of the group learn to help plan, and take part in, a series of small-group discussions that deal with topics agreed on by the participants.
2. They learn more about themselves—how they are seen by colearners, how their participation affects others, what some of the educational problems and needs of a group are, and how to deal with them.
3. They learn how to help others in a group-learning situation.
4. They learn how to develop disciplined freedom of expression.

5. They learn, through experience, what helps and what hinders productive learning through group discussion

6. They learn, through experience, group educational skills and concepts such as: goal setting, interpersonal communication, evaluation, consensus, disciplined observing, leadership, focusing of topics, and discovering and meeting educational needs.

C. How does a participation-training group differ from the usual discussion groups?

Some characteristics of a participation-training group mark it as distinct from many traditional study-discussion groups:

1. Training sessions (see Chapter 5) are supervised by a leader who is usually called a "trainer." The trainer does not serve as the discussion leader, and ideally he does not serve as a source of information on topics that are discussed. His main job is to help the participants become an effective learning group.

2. The process of talking together as well as the content of the discussion is used as a source of conscious learning.

3. Discussions are led by trained participants who volunteer.

4. Participants and volunteer discussion leaders are co-responsible for the success of each discussion; learning to work together effectively is one of the purposes of the training.

5. Topics and related learning goals are determined by the participants.

6. The trainer interrupts the discussion at crucial times to help the group analyze its process and procedures.

7. Each session ends with an open appraisal (called a critique) in which participants assess their joint effort, identify obstacles, and plan to improve the learning situation.

SOME DIFFERENCES BETWEEN A USUAL DISCUSSION GROUP AND A PARTICIPATION-TRAINING GROUP

ELEMENTS COMPARED	PARTICIPATION-TRAINING GROUP	DISCUSSION GROUP
(1) Trainer	A specialist who helps the group realize effective participation	No trainer
(2) Discussion Leader	A participant who volunteers to serve as designated leader of discussion for one or two sessions	Often a teacher-leader, an expert in the subject being discussed
(3) Leader's Job	To help direct discussion along the line participants as a group decide to pursue	To direct discussion along lines he feels to be most helpful; to offer subject information when he feels it necessary
(4) Group Participant's Job	a. To learn to share in leadership by being a responsible group member b. To help self and other participants struggle with learning problems common to the participants c. To learn to understand self better as a learner d. To help other participants understand themselves better as learners	a. To follow the leader b. To learn about the subject matter

ELEMENTS COMPARED	PARTICIPATION-TRAINING GROUP	DISCUSSION GROUP
(5) Topics	Topics *always* chosen by group consensus; topics arise from interests and needs recognized by participants	Topics often chosen by participants, with the advice and approval of a leader; often chosen in advance by leader or defined by a resource book
(6) Goal-setting	Participants learn to define their own learning goals for each session; goals are visible and open to change; goals in terms of attainable outcomes are sought	Seldom has visible goals; goals are usually teaching goals developed by leader. Such goals are often stated as tasks which define content to be covered
(7) Use Made of Resources	Discussion often centers on problems common to participants; resources used as means to understanding and solving learning problems	Discussion often centers on issues found in resource materials or defined by resource person

D. How many meetings should be necessary?

Many successful training groups meet once each week. Usually from four to five months of weekly sessions are necessary to achieve the goals of the training program. Meetings scheduled two weeks apart are *much* less effective than weekly meetings.

In scheduling training sessions, trainers tend to organize a participation-training program that consists of only four to six sessions. This is a mistake. A weekend of concentrated sessions is usually not enough time and neither is a series of four to six weekly sessions. It is not sufficient merely to illustrate or talk about the mechanics of participation training. The training experience must last long enough for participants to do some reflecting, to discover some of their needs and problems, and to develop sufficient freedom together to allow them to experience the learning desired. We do not learn to be responsible participants by merely hearing our responsibilities described. After we know what responsibilities are involved, we really learn by practicing over a long period of time.

The classic defense for a short-cut series of sessions goes something like this:

> This group is different from other groups. These principles have been in use for years. The participants already know each other. They have worked together for years. They already have freedom of expression and they are used to developing programs. Besides, they wouldn't hold still for more than three or four sessions. They already have had a lot of experience "in this sort of thing." Most of them are already leaders. Also, they have read all the latest books on leadership, group dynamics, and group participation. One of them is a personnel man and several of them are schoolteachers, intelligent people who need only a couple of sessions to pick up these techniques.

This kind of reasoning wrongly assumes that what is important is the learning of mechanical procedures and techniques. It falsely assumes that intelligent people who read books on leadership and participation and who can use some technical words can in some magical way translate knowledge into experience. It falsely assumes that persons who already know each other socially have already learned to communicate as well as possible. These assumptions usually are not valid.

Many different time patterns have been used for scheduling training sessions. Below are listed four approaches. For each approach some indication is given of an approximate length of time required for the group members to become a working team. In actual practice, the speed with which discussion teamwork and insights develop will depend upon such variable factors as: the motivation of individual participants; the skill of the trainer; the regularity with which participants attend sessions; the length, frequency, and continuity of training sessions; the willingness of participants to trust the trainer.

1. A weekend plus weekly meetings. The training program starts with a number of sessions concentrated in a short space of time. Motivation is preserved and strengthened for later sessions if the participants can work through the mechanics and initial cursory survey of topics in a series of weekend sessions.

Two types of initial weekend programs are possible: (1) the retreat type, in which the group goes to a conference center or a camp for an away-from-home experience; and (2) the stay-at-home type, in which participants attend sessions throughout the day and return to their own homes in the evenings. The first of these two types is usually considered the better because participants can eat their meals together, share in evening recreational activities, and talk about their developing teamwork and new insights. If the participants retire to their own homes each evening, the weekend experience they share is usually less effective; they live in two worlds.

Nevertheless, starting the training group with "stay-at-home weekend" sessions is more effective than starting with weekly sessions. A full weekend meeting plus six to eight weekly meetings usually provides sufficient time to enable a group to become an effective learning team. An example of a weekend schedule is given in Appendix A, together with notes on each session, for the convenience of trainers who wish to plan weekend sessions.

2. Five Consecutive Evenings Plus Weekly Sessions. Conducting five 2- to $2\frac{1}{2}$-hour training sessions on consecutive evenings is another useful way of concentrating the early sessions. Usually a minimum of eight to ten weekly follow-up sessions of about $2\frac{1}{2}$ hours each would then be required to enable the group to become an effective learning team.

3. Semiweekly Sessions. If two sessions (each of $2\frac{1}{2}$ to 3 hours in length) are conducted each week, the group will usually need a minimum of six to eight weeks to become an effective learning team.

4. Weekly Sessions. One of the popular schedules is that of the single session conducted once each week. Usually a group with this schedule requires from fifteen to twenty $2\frac{1}{2}$-hour meetings to become an effective learning team.

Thirty- to forty-five-minute sessions are not long enough unless the group can begin the operation with a concentrated series of weekend sessions, or some equivalent. The observer's report, the shared verbal critique, topic selection, goal setting, and training interruptions (if done effectively) consume so much time in early sessions that participants become unduly frustrated if only 45 minutes are available. Certain adaptations can be made, however, to incorporate some training-group procedures into short-term adult classes.

For information on weekend sessions see Appendix A.

E. How long should the meetings last?

It is best to have from 1½ to 2 hours available for each session. This makes it possible for the participants to talk informally before and after the discussion, and to plan carefully for the succeeding session. A fairly effective, but hurried, training session can be conducted if from 1 to 1½ hours are available.

F. Where should meetings be held?

Training sessions can be held in private homes, but experience shows the advantage of holding meetings on neutral ground, where nobody is the host. Participants seem to feel more able and willing to pursue the learning task when they are not in the roles of host and guests.

G. How important is regular attendance?

The operation and purpose of a training group are different from those of a class that meets to hear a lecture and ask questions. Participants in a training group do more than discuss information and opinions. They also examine their own relationships with the other learners in the group. For this reason each session builds upon the last one and the effect is cumulative. Regular attendance is, therefore, necessary. Participants who can attend only half the meetings should not attend at all. Regular attendance at the first six or eight sessions is particularly important.

H. How large should a group be?

Training groups have varied in size from eight to more than twenty persons. Groups of ten to fifteen participants are usually considered optimal in size, small enough to be seated around a table—an arrangement in which all participants are in eye contact.

I. Who should be members of the group?

The composition of the group depends upon the purpose of the training as envisioned by an *organizational adminis-trator*. For example, a training group can be organized for leadership training *per se* and the participants would be different from those assembled for another purpose.

In general, all people who work or learn together, or who work with groups of people, can profit from a training-group experience. Government groups, agricultural groups, military and industrial groups, church groups, and hospital and public service institutions are some examples of insti-tutions whose personnel could profit by this training. Often husbands and wives find it particularly valuable to share a training-group experience.

J. What is the difference between group-participation train-ing and leadership training?

In its most significant application, group-participation train-ing is a program not only for training leaders, but also for training those who are the so-called members of the group. This training is comprehensive. It affects all participants in the group, as well as its leadership.

Group-participation training offers sound educational ex-periences concerning each role—that of the leader, the co-leader, the observer, the recorder, the resource person, the group participants, and the trainer. Each participant, includ-ing the leader, can be carefully trained to function in each particular role of the training group.

This kind of training broadens the base of leadership be-cause participants trained in all the roles become less fear-ful of taking on the job of leader or any other group re-sponsibility. In fact, more and more participants volunteer for the leadership role after the training progresses and they see that leadership is not as difficult as it might have seemed

17

earlier. However, no one is pressed to take the leadership role or any other role if he does not wish to do so.

In this training the leader is also placed in the proper perspective. He is not looked upon as a specially trained group dominator, but rather as a participant who has volunteered to carry out a particular role of participation.

K. Will slow learners hold the group back?

Held back from what? Persons who ask this question often assume that the only task of participants is to "cover" subject-matter facts. Some may be able to memorize or explain facts and opinions better than others, but learning to understand the topic is not the only important task of a learning group. The topics discussed are important, but a training group has a second and equally important task—to explore topics so that its members can also learn more about (a) how they relate to others in groups, (b) how they can learn to help themselves and others as learners, and (c) how they can help improve this and other group situations in which they take part. In this kind of learning, most participants are fairly "slow" learners.

We are in a real sense concerned about the subject under study and discussion chiefly as it relates to us and what is happening to us as we associate with fellow learners in this learning program. How we react to conflicting views, how we present our point of view, how we take and offer criticism, how well we listen to, weigh, and evaluate others' ideas, how we deal with our prejudices and opinions and those of others, and how we handle a new idea are all important factors in participation training. We are indeed concerned about learning "subjects" but not subjects in isolation. We are concerned first about people and we must make an effort to make the subject the servant of the learner—to help the adult learner make use of *all* resources of a learning situation which contribute toward his maturation.

The speed of learning must be assessed in more than one area of accomplishment. How fast we learn the subject must be related to how well we learn it; but further, while studying a subject, we are concerned with becoming trained to use the total experience gained through intra- and interpersonal relationships. With this dual approach we can realize a higher return in maturation for the time and effort expended.

L. Participation training is not group psychotherapy.

Discussion training should not be thought of as a form of group psychotherapy. Several characteristics mark the distinction between group psychotherapy and participation training.

Participation trainers have no treatment function. In psychotherapy groups, the therapist often interprets patients' motivations and accounts for present problems by tracing back through their past life experiences to discover the underlying causes of individual behavior and unconscious motives. The educational trainer does not do these things.

The therapist helps persons analyze their personality structure (psychodynamics). The educational trainer does not do this. In the training group the educational emphasis is on a problem common to the group, and there is no analysis of individual personalities. Evaluation in a training group is confined to factors in the present group situation. Emphasis is placed on present relationships between participants (sociodynamics), not on the workings of individual personalities (psychodynamics).

M. How should the group be recruited?

Trainers and administrators are usually faced with an initial decision: Should the group be publicized and organized on the basis of a preset provisional subject area—some common interest or problem area known to exist? Or on the basis of some subject it is thought they "need" to know? This is often an effective organizing principle even though it implies that all sessions will deal with the given subject area. Actually, the group participants should be made responsible for deciding on the common problems and needs with which they wish to deal. Therefore, even though participants are originally organized for a provisional, agreed-on subject area, they should not be constrained to stay strictly within that area.

An alternate decision is to organize the group with the understanding that they *must* stay within a given subject area. This method has worked many times, but it assumes that the participants do or will recognize that there are real problems and needs (not just an interest) in that area. It does not allow for flexibility to shift the emphasis when unforeseen needs are discovered. This approach limits the potentiality of the group; also it can mean that the participants will have to abandon directions to which their motivation might impel them.

The question often boils down to this: (a) Do we wish to take advantage of the readiness and motivation that develops in the learning situation? or (b) Should we hold to a predetermined course because this is what some expert thinks they need? Needs originally recognized often change, so, if a program is to be fitted to our needs as we discover them, we may have to abandon the subjects prearranged in logical order. It is usually better to follow a psychological order in studying subject matter, which is the order in which learners are most able and willing to discover significance. A *logical* order meets the needs of teachers who must explain. A *psychological* order meets the needs of volunteer adult learners who discover largely on their own terms.

The "imposed subject" approach is not always ineffective; but it does establish conditions which can interfere with the development of creative learning experiences.

A second early decision concerns the best way to contact the potential participants. If a defined group already exists and is willing to become a training group, there is no problem. Otherwise, there is the problem of whether to contact certain persons individually or to issue an open invitation. If the group is not organized for the express purpose of training known leaders, then it is usually helpful to issue an open invitation, within the sponsoring organization, in order to avoid the charge that the group is for certain chosen persons. This is a charge to be avoided if the training program eventually is to be extended throughout an institutional organization.

N. Should there be an organizational meeting?

Usually it is best to schedule an organizational meeting for all potential participants. At this meeting the trainer should explain clearly:

1. the purpose of the training program
2. the manner in which the sessions will be conducted
3. the educational conditions or principles of the program
4. anticipated outcomes

Most of the persons attending the meeting will have little or no understanding of the nature of participation training as a productive means of learning. In fact, some persons will be hostile to any system that differs from the one they were exposed to as students in formal educational programs, a system which employed memorization and regurgitation. This position should be understood by the trainer and deftly handled during the discussion if it arises. Tact is necessary; it is not advisable to go too far into these basic differences. (The candidates for the training program will begin to see the differences and appreciate them as they progress in the participation-training program.)

The participants should agree on the dates to be scheduled for the meetings. If the group is to meet weekly, it would be well for participants to commit themselves to at least six or eight sessions, after which they can decide whether to proceed with more meetings. If the program is to begin with a series of concentrated weekend training sessions, participants should commit themselves to the entire weekend.

O. What materials are necessary for conducting these sessions?

Two kinds of materials are usually helpful to participants. First, there should be informational materials and reference books appropriate to the topics to be discussed in the sessions. Second, each participant should have access to a copy of this manual.

Chapter 2

Roles of Participant

A. *Introduction*

In developing a participation-training program, participants serve in one or more of six roles: (1) discussion leader (and coleader), (2) observer, (3) recorder, (4) group participant, (5) resource person, or (6) trainer. In smaller groups the roles of coleader, recorder, and discussion leader are sometimes combined and all the functions are handled by the discussion leader, but in large discussion groups a person is usually needed for each of the three roles.

B. *Brief Description of Roles*

The *discussion leader* for a given session or series of sessions is a participant who volunteers to accept the primary responsibility for helping the participants work together effectively as they discuss their topic and try to achieve their mutual goals. He coordinates and facilitates; he is not a teacher or a boss. He helps the group participants decide and do what they want to do as a group. A *coleader* sometimes is needed to help the discussion leader. In large discussion groups (15 to 20 persons), the coleader helps the discussion leader coordinate discussion. His is a service role, much like the discussion leader's. Some groups combine the coleader and the *recorder*. In this situation, the coleader makes a record of the developing discussion on a chalkboard or large chart pad in addition to carrying out his responsibilities as assistant in the leadership role.

The *observer* for a given session is a participant who volunteers to watch how the group works as a discussion team and to report his observations when called upon—usually in the critique period after the discussion. He does not blame individuals, but objectively reports what he saw happening in the group so that the participants will have evidence to use in discussing their progress.

The *group participants* are the persons who discuss the topic and for whom the discussion exists. All others—discussion leader, coleader, recorder—are servants who help the group participants accomplish their objectives.

The *trainer* is the specially trained person who helps volunteer discussion leaders become more effective in their roles, observers to become more effective observers, and group participants to become more responsible group members. He does not serve as the discussion leader; he helps the group become an effective discussion team.

The trainer has been schooled in the nature and use of adult educational procedures and processes and he knows how to teach them to other persons. He may be a professional adult educator or a layman. The trainer is not a permanent fixture in a group. His job is to train others (discussion leaders, group participants, observers, recorders, and resource persons) and when he finishes the training job, he puts the group on its own.

The *resource person* is one who has had special training and/or significant experience in the subject that is discussed at a given meeting. He is called on for information at various times when needed. Often he is not a regular member of the group. He is asked to attend those meetings at which his unique contribution to the learning process is needed.

C. Duties of Each Participant

1. The Discussion Leader

The discussion leader for a given session or series of sessions is the one who volunteers to accept primary responsibility for helping coordinate the interaction of the group participants, for helping them work together effectively as they discuss their topic and try to achieve their mutual goals. He is not necessarily the person who knows the most about the topic. The discussion leader serves the group; he helps the group decide what they want to do together and does not attempt to lead the group to accept his own or someone else's "acceptable" conclusion. He fades into the background whenever the group is able to work together without his assistance.

In this kind of learning experience the usual sharp distinction is not drawn between the discussion leader and the other participants. Here the discussion leader is a participant who has volunteered to assume a specialized role in the learning adventure. He is not a teacher in the usual academic sense. He has some knowledge about the process of learning implicit in participation training and he participates by practicing what he knows in the group.

The discussion leader in this kind of group participation is not in the position of the teacher in the usual class-teacher situation. The group does not come to a meeting to see what the discussion leader has to say. The kind of leadership described here puts the responsibility for learning where it belongs—on every person in the group. In a similar fashion the group participants, the observer, etc., are also trained in this kind of learning experience and they participate by playing their unique roles.

Responsibility for the success of this enterprise is shared by *all* participants. Each person knows his role and the contribution he must make if it is to result in a fruitful learning experience.

Shared leadership cannot be described wholly by giving a complete list of responsibilities. This kind of leadership involves fundamental feelings and beliefs about the essential worth of each person in the group. Without these beliefs and feelings the discussion leader may perform the listed responsibilities mechanically and to little avail.

The major responsibilities of the volunteer discussion leader in participation training are as follows:

Before the Meeting

    a. To read suggested resource materials on the topic that is to be discussed.

    b. To review the tentative topic question, goals, and outline that the group developed for each coming session. If the group decided on a topic only, the discussion leader can develop suggested goals and discussion outline to present to the group.[1]

    c. To develop some questions which *might* be useful in starting the discussion and bringing out all sides of the question.

    d. To check the physical setting of the discussion to make sure that light and ventilation are adequate and that necessary physical properties are available.

During the Discussion:

    a. To submit the tentative topic, goals, and outline to the group for possible adjustment. Allow time for adjustment. Remember that these are the group's responsibility, not the discussion leader's. At first the group will be slow to accept this responsibility.

    b. To introduce the topic briefly, suggesting its significance, and present a question to start the discussion.

    c. To remain neutral. Particularly in early sessions the discussion leader should not express his opinion on the topic. When asked for an opinion, the questions can be reflected back to the group participants.

    d. To encourage free expression and balanced participation. He must try to draw in a maximum number of

---

[1]See Chapter 3 for guidance in this procedure.

participants without embarrassing those who seem to prefer to be silent. He opens doors without pushing people through them. He makes opportunities for various points of view to be heard. Unbalanced participation results when one or a few persons are dominating the discussion. He makes an effort to prevent domination, but remembers that the observer's report and the critique will eventually deal with the problem of domination.

e. To help the group work as a purposeful team. This task requires the discussion leader to alert the group when he thinks they are off the topic. He must remember, however, that sometimes the group may decide that a digression is more important than the agreed-on topic.

f. To help group participants communicate with each other. When a contribution is overlooked or not dealt with, it must be brought to the attention of the group. Overeager participants who have not yet developed sensitivity to others' feelings and ideas often do not listen to contributions that interfere with what they wish to say. Thus, they try to disregard the unheard ideas. The leader will help the group deal with contributions as they are made. He will rephrase contributions he thinks participants have not understood. He may ask for clarification when he feels it necessary. These tasks the discussion leader must perform until group participants take over the responsibility for doing them.

g. To record main points of the discussion on the easel or chalkboard, if there is no recorder or coleader, or to help with suggestions for the recorder if there is one.

h. To try to keep the whole discussion going in a purposeful manner. Sometimes a little pressure is indicated; sometimes a relaxed atmosphere is better.

After the Discussion:

a. To summarize the discussion, if a summary would be helpful.

b. To call for the observer's report if the observer's role is used. Otherwise, the trainer may be asked how he wishes the critique to be started.

c. After the critique, to help the group plan the next session (arranging for topic, goals, outline, and volunteer discussion leader[s] and observer).

2. The Coleader and/or Recorder

If the group has 12 or more participants, it may be advantageous to use a coleader. Usually the coleader helps the leader coordinate the discussion—a service role much like the discussion leader's. Sometimes, his major responsibility is serving as recorder, assisting in other leadership tasks when he is not occupied with the task of recording. He makes a record of the developing discussion on a blackboard or large chart pad.

There are two popular ways of recording a discussion. One might be called *selective recording.* In this method the recorder jots down what he considers to be the major points of the discussion. In *comprehensive recording* as many contributions as possible are recorded by the recorder. The latter approach requires the use of much blackboard space or many sheets of butcher paper for each discussion. Therefore, most training groups use the selective style of recording, with the understanding that group participants are to indicate points they wish to have recorded whenever the coleader or recorder fails to put them down.

The selective recorder tries to write up, in short form, the significant ideas or points that are contributed during the discussion. He usually does not write complete sentences for thoughts expressed, because it is easier to jot down phrases that symbolize these ideas. His writing must be legible and the condensation understandable.

Suggestions for the Recorder:

a. He should not try to record the discussion by forcing it into a formal outline.
b. He should avoid noting the names of those who make the contributions.
c. When the recorder feels it advisable during the discussion, he may ask whether he is recording in a helpful way. Group participants must accept responsibility in the recording process, if they feel it necessary.

d. If he records with crayon on a large chart pad, he will need to hang up finished pages at various times during the discussion. Thus, he should have thumbtacks or pieces of masking tape (1-inch or 2-inch strips) prepared before the discussion starts for hanging them. The recorder must be considerate and will not hang these sheets where the tape or thumbtacks will damage wallpaper, paint, or woodwork.

e. Customarily the recorder's role is a service role and not that of a verbal contributor to the content of the discussion. Usually he has enough to do recording other's contributions.

f. The recorder's job may and usually should be passed around. Different persons may wish to assume this responsibility.

3. The Group Participant

The effectiveness of the discussion depends as much upon the group participants—their acceptance of responsibilities—as upon the discussion leader. In this program of learning, the group participants come to share a large part of the responsibilities that are listed for the discussion leader. As group participants take on these responsibilities, the discussion leader has less and less to do. Finally, all participants share in leadership and the leader has few things which only he must do. Here are the major responsibilities of each group participant:

Before the Meeting:

The group participant should prepare in advance to contribute to the discussion. This usually means reading and thinking about the topic and its social or personal significance.

During the Discussion:

a. If necessary, the participant should help adjust the tentative topic, goals, and outline at the start of the discussion. It is the group participants' discussion. The discussion leader is present only to keep things moving,

29

to coordinate, to serve the needs of the group, to get the group participants to assume more and more responsibility for the success of the learning program.

b. He must share his ideas and feelings during the discussion. He is trying to understand better his own ideas and others' and to build more adequate understandings. He is not there to prove somebody else wrong. Good discussion involves a degree of conflict, but is fundamentally cooperative. It should produce mutual understanding, not necessarily agreement. Often the mutual understanding involves understandings of disagreement.

c. He should help other group participants take part by giving them opportunities to talk.

d. When other participants are having trouble understanding each other, he cannot sit smugly back and think he is responsible only for himself. He should assist others to communicate, without showing off.

e. He can alert the group when he feels the discussion is "off the topic." He should help the group decide whether the "off-topic" discussion is more important than discussion of the agreed-on topic.

f. He should listen actively and indicate his interest. If he is *not* interested, then perhaps the group should know how he feels about it. He should avoid half-listening, which often results when he is planning what he is going to say next.

g. He should build on contributions that precede his, if possible. In this way he can help prevent others from ignoring someone's idea.

h. He should try to help other participants work out conflicts and problem situations that occur, instead of depending upon the designated discussion leader to do it. Each one should learn to help others without being ostentatious.

i. He may help the chalkboard recorder to phrase ideas concisely, if the recorder needs help. The object is not necessarily to reach and record agreement, but to explore and record various ideas.

After the Discussion:

a. The group participant should take part actively in the critique evaluation.

b. He should help work out a meaningful discussion unit for the next discussion. This may include wording the topic, suggesting goals, and developing an outline of appropriate discussion tasks.

4. The Observer

The observer for a particular session volunteers to watch how the group functions as a discussion team. He jots down his observations so that he can report them to the group when called upon. In the critique after the discussion, all participants discuss the observations and attempt to identify the obstacles they encountered and ways of overcoming them.

There are two styles of observing: comprehensive observing and selective observing. In comprehensive observing, the observer attempts to describe chronologically a maximum number of the observable process factors during the discussion. In selective observing, the observer has a check list of selected discussion characteristics which he uses to help him classify certain aspects of the discussion. Here is a sample list of characteristics:

a. spontaneity of participation
b. balanced participation
c. emotional atmosphere
d. dependence upon the discussion leader
e. helping others communicate
f. decision-making procedures
g. factors that blocked progress toward goals
h. clarity of tasks and goals
i. building upon others' contributions
j. overlooking others' contributions
k. quality of listening

Suggestions for Observers:

a. The observer should avoid referring to a person by name in his report.
b. He should report what he saw happening, not what he

thinks should have happened. The group may wish, however, to discuss this latter aspect.

c. He should not keep a record of the subject content of the discussion. This is done by the recorder.

d. He should sit where he can see the faces of most of the participants.

e. He should remember that what he reports may be attacked for being inaccurate. People do not see situations alike. What he sees honestly is valid for him. All the argument and proof-citing to the contrary does not change the way the reporter saw and interpreted the situation; what he saw is the evidence that the group should deal with, regardless of whether they agree with what he saw. If he is careful and objective, it is likely that he will see more about the process than the other participants, since they are busy in another area.

5. The Resource Person

The role of the resource person is often misunderstood. Too often a person with special training and experience is asked to a discussion-training meeting to make a 30-minute speech to initiate the discussion. Or he may listen to a few minutes of discussion and then give a speech, which tapers off into a speech-forum with questions from the group.

The object of the discussion should not be to discuss a speech or to furnish material upon which the resource person is to build a speech. The group should carefully plan the discussion around a topical problem about which participants already have some information and/ or experience; and then, in the light of specialized information which they may need, seek an appropriate resource person to answer questions the participants have raised or might raise. *The focus is on the planned discussion, not on the resource person's information.* Resource persons must be oriented to their job before they serve.

Suggestions for Resource Persons:

a. The resource person will be asked to give information and to offer his informed opinions at various points during the discussion. He should not make long speeches; he should try to fit his information to the needs of the group.
b. He should avoid the detailed background of theory which substantiates his answers. To him, as a specialist, a scholar, or a professional, these may be important. He should not try to make the group participants into specialists by giving them a short course in his specialty.
c. Participants are supposed to ask for information when it is needed, but often they do not know when it is needed. No doubt the resource person could add substantially to every point that is made in the discussion. But he must remember that it is the group's discussion. At some points, he might indicate that he has something to say, but generally speaking, he should *wait until he is called upon for information.*

6. The Trainer

The trainer's tools and tasks are described in detail in Chapter 4; in Chapter 5 several sections are concerned with the relation of the trainer to the other participants. Here it is necessary only to characterize the relationship of the trainer with the other participants in general terms.

The trainer is a teacher who concentrates his teaching efforts at the level of group processes and procedures in order to help participants become more effective learners and colearners. He is concerned with improving communication, self-understanding, decision-making, and group operation. He is not to serve as a source of information about the subject being discussed.

A popular false image of the effective trainer depicts him as a godlike seer, aware of all the psychological forces unleashed in the group and their appropriate technical terminology—one who sits in splendid isolation, withholding valuable insights with a haughty smirk because he believes group members must learn everything through painful experience without outside help. If outside help were not necessary, there would be little need for a trainer.

Participants must discover new insights for themselves. No one can learn for another. The trainer's function is to spare participants needless frustration, not to create it. He needs to be seen and trusted as a helper who is functioning also as a learner.

Few groups, however, learn much about discussion group processes and procedures without experiencing some frustration. This frustration is not usually caused by the trainer, although he is often blamed because the group needs a scapegoat. In the trainer-participant relationship, it is not so much what the trainer does to help us that is important; it is rather (a) what the participants think he did and (b) why they think he did it. Effective trainers are seldom defensive, because they recognize that their actions are perceived differently by different persons.

To be most effective, a trainer should have had experience as a group participant in a learning group. He should understand his role thoroughly and clearly know how his role differs from that of a leader.

D. Effective Group Conditions

The group conditions listed below describe the basis for the effective operation of a participation-training group. They sum up both the basic characteristics of a successful discussion group and the means by which success is attained.

1. Shared Planning. Participants share in developing both discussion tasks and goals; decisions on these are made by consensus.

2. Shared Appraisal. Participants share in developing each discussion openly, giving each other information about how each reacted to different events and situations in the discussion. Efforts are made to identify obstacles to effective discussion and growth of individual understanding, and plans are made to overcome these obstacles.

3. Free, Voluntary Expression. An atmosphere of freedom is developed in which participants can learn together without embarrassment; participants are not pressured to talk or to volunteer as discussion leader or observer. Active verbal participation directed toward the achieving of mutual goals is encouraged.

4. Communication. Emphasis is placed on understanding each other's different points of view and on exploring all viewpoints rather than on proving each other right or wrong. This involves learning to *listen effectively* as well as to talk. Responsibility for effective communication is shared by all participants.

5. Mutual Acceptance as Persons. Participants come to recognize that each other person is a unique individual whom each must respect, encourage, and support but with whom he need not necessarily agree. Respect for each other's feelings is maintained. Development of free expression depends upon acceptance of each other by participants.

Chapter 3

Elements of Structure:

Topic, Goals, and Outline

A. *Introduction*

Three elements help provide structure and purpose for each discussion: the topic, the goals, and the outline. The participants develop and use these elements in each session, with minimal guidance from the trainer. Only after we learn what these elements are and how they can be aligned to work together, can we use them effectively as means to an educational end.

B. *Topic*

Choosing a topic is usually the first step in planning a discussion.[1] A good discussion topic is an educational problem stated as a question. Learning groups should state the topic as a question not answerable by yes or no (see chapter 5, section U). Groups searching for an appropriate topic to explore often find it helpful to use a two-step procedure. First, several possible areas of interest should be identified so that participants will have alternative topic areas from which to choose. From these, the group comes to an agree-

---

[1]Sometimes groups wish to begin with goals. Knowledge of desired outcomes *can* lead to topic selection as a second step.

ment on a broad topic area, based on problems which the participants recognize and have in common.

Second, participants can tentatively phrase several topics within the chosen area and then agree on one topic. At this point it is important for participants to remember that they probably will reword and refine the topic question after they develop tentative goals and outlines. The topic that is agreed on is yet to be considered tentative in form. (See section E of this chapter, "Focusing the Topic.")

Beginning groups overlook the significance of carefully wording the topic. Instead they tend to word their topics hastily, often expressing them vaguely: "the world situation," "the need for a youth center," or "improving family life." These obscure phrases and themes obviously do not give specific direction for focused discussion; they are really "topic areas" instead of topics. Wording the topic clearly in the form of a question, not answerable by a simple yes or no, has been found to be the most satisfactory form.

What is a significant topic? In participation training, significant topics are usually those which relate to our own beliefs, feelings, and personal experiences, those which involve most of us enough to activate freedom of expression.

C. Goals

After agreeing on a tentative topic question, the group members seek to identify some provisional goals to which they can give their assent. Goals express desired results—the outcomes which group participants hope to achieve through this educational experience. In learning groups, effective goals[2] are:

1. expressed in terms of desired changes in participants' behavior, feelings, or understandings

---

[2]Written goals usually appear in one of two forms: (1) in the infinitive form: "to improve our . . .," "to understand more about . . .," "to appreciate more fully . . .," "to increase understanding of . . .," etc.; (2) in the noun form: "the improvement of . . .," "increased understanding of . . .," etc.

2. attainable
3. specific
4. shared by the participants
5. made visible to the group in written form

Whenever possible, participants should express their discussion goals in terms of desirable changes in themselves. These kinds of goals are necessary if the effect of discussion is later to be evaluated realistically.

Participants in beginning groups tend to avoid setting goals that call for changes in their feelings or behavior. They prefer to set goals that call for increased understandings, or for lists and word packages of possible solutions. Such immediate verbal outcomes can be summarized conveniently at the end of a discussion, enabling the participants to say that they have achieved their goal. The last section of this chapter is devoted to an explanation of this dilemma.

▶ Avoidance of Goals Relating to Behavior Change

Groups avoid setting goals that call for individual change by choosing topics which seem unrelated to individual problems and needs. These topics, for instance, may call for exploration of national or community problems, thus allowing participants to keep their own real educational problems and needs at a distance.

Another common way of avoiding goals relating to behavior changes is by using, instead, goals worded "to identify . . . ," "to explore . . . ," or "to learn more about. . . ." These may be legitimate substitutes for effective goals in early sessions, but they will not serve for long because they indicate only what is to happen during the session rather than as a result of it.

Some of the obstacles which appear when a trainer is trying in the early discussion to help a group set goals relating to behavior change are as follows:

1. participants hesitate to pledge themselves to make an effort to change unless they know and trust their colearners
2. participants may not be able to agree, even generally, on individual changes that are desirable beyond changes of understanding
3. participants cannot always anticipate a need to change in a given area. Perhaps certain information needs to be explored and better understood. Perhaps changes are not needed or perceived as needed.

Realistic, shared goal-setting presupposes that participants recognize problems and needs, which, however, are often not discovered until after several sessions have passed.

D. *The Outline*

Having selected a tentative topic and tentative goals, the participants next turn to devising an outline. The discussion outline is the plan of attack to be used to reach the goal(s). It defines both the specific nature of the content of the desired discussion and the sequence of tasks to be followed. The outline may appear on the blackboard or in handouts in one of three forms:

1. as a series of subtopic questions
2. as a series of key words or phrases
3. as tasks (similar to goal statements).

The following examples illustrate the three forms of discussion outlines. In (A) the outline appears as questions; in (B) it appears as phrases and words; in (C) it is expressed as goal-like tasks.

EXAMPLE A:

Topic: How can we express acceptance[3] more effectively in our home life?

---

[3]See Glossary of Terms.

Goal: To express acceptance more effectively in our home life

Outline: What do we mean by acceptance?

With which home-life situation do we deal, and what are our problems in expressing acceptance?

What are some solutions to try?

(Topic and goal same as in A)

Outline: Meaning of acceptance

Difficult home-life acceptance situations

Solutions

(Topic and goal same as in A)

Outline: To explore what we mean by acceptance

To identify our home-life problems of expressing acceptance

To seek ways to express acceptance more effectively

The use of questions in the outline, as in (A), is usually helpful and explicit. The use of single words and phrases is often vague so that participants tend to assume that they agree on the tasks when actually they may not. When outline items are expressed as goal-like statements (as in Example C), they describe the definite nature and steps of the discussion that is to take place. This is probably why the question and task forms are more often used.

Whichever form is used, the outline of discussion tasks should be arranged in the most convenient way to help the group achieve its goal(s). Tasks are, after all, only instrumental activities that lead to achieving goals.

Tasks are often seen as one type of goal, because the completing of a task can be a form of goal-achievement. Thus, some educators prefer to think of tasks as task goals.

E. Focusing the Topic: Advance Planning

To use the topic, goals, and outline effectively the participants as a team must learn to manipulate them creatively. Each of these three elements needs to be adjusted to the other two. Thus, participants can waste much time trying to state the discussion topic in final form before tentative goals and outline have been suggested. Final decision on any one of the three elements should be suspended until all three have been related and adjusted to each other.

Participants often say, "We should limit our topic." One effective way to limit a topic, or discussion problem, is as follows: (1) First, the group gets a tentative version of *all three* elements visually before the group. (2) *Then* they focus the topic by adjusting the elements. Potential points of focus may be found in topic questions, in goals, and in the tasks of the outline. Some of the points of focus are identified in the following discussion unit. They are enclosed in brackets with alternative wording.

EXAMPLE

[employers]

TOPIC: How can [people] express acceptance [more]
[we]

effectively [in our daily work?]
[in home life?]
[in church life?]

GOALS: (1) To learn ways to express acceptance effectively

(2) To express our acceptance [more] effectively

[in our daily work]
[in our home life]
[in our church life]

41

OUTLINE: To explore what [is meant by] acceptance
                         [we mean by]

To identify and explore [some] common prob-
                        [our]

lems of expressing acceptance in   [our daily work]
                                    [our home life]
                                    [our church]

To seek ways [people] can better express ac-
             [we]

          in [our] daily work
ceptance   in [our] home life
          in [our] church life

One version of the topic is stated so that it contains a potential image of the participants doing something about their problem.[4] The other two versions—employers and people—require them to talk about other persons. If the learning group is to discuss common problems and meet individual needs, its topic should express the *participants' problems*. The topic can be focused more sharply by certain choices which would align the problem with the need of the participants. Obviously the group could make the topic as specific as they desire.

After provisional topics, goals, and outline tasks have been developed is the time to go back and limit the topic, which limitation may in turn cause goals and tasks in the outline to be readjusted and made more specific. This is the focusing procedure; it requires participants to plan together creatively while suspending final decisions on topic, goal and outline.

---

[4]One way to avoid personalizing a topic is to state it in a passive instead of active form: "How can acceptance be expressed effectively?" This form of topic emphasize the abstract concept of acceptance, which lends itself to authorities, letting them de battle for us. Authoritative information is necessary, but is best used to illuminate ou own feelings and ideas that arise out of our experience. The desirable end is a more enlightened choice in the business of living, not just an intellectual understanding o resource materials.

Goal 1 in the example above does not express an outcome in terms of changes in participants. The goal as stated would be achieved if the meeting produced a list of ways in which improvement could take place. Thus, goal 1 might well be used as a task item in the outline, because it defines an activity to be accomplished during the meeting; it is essentially a task statement. The difference between goals 1 and 2 is the difference between (a) setting out to compile and memorize ideas and words, and (b) stating our intentions to try to change, to put ideas into practice.

In this example, potential points of focus are enclosed in brackets. Obviously a group has many opportunities to focus the topic by adjusting the tasks to specific problems and to the experience and needs of the participants.

1. Use of the Focusing Procedure.

We do not refine and adjust topics, goals, and outlines in order to make them look academically respectable, nor to exalt the mechanical elements of this sort of learning process. The justification for focusing is that it can lead to a more meaningful and effective educational experience. A valuable by-product of the focusing process is that participants can learn more about the identification of real educational problems and needs. This is the beginning of productive learning.

2. Avoidance of focusing.

We participants search for increased understandings, for personal meaning, and for some kind of expression of our unique selves. But until we learn to trust our co-learners, we resist efforts to focus openly on our individual educational problems and needs. We often avoid coming to terms with this basic issue:

a. by resisting efforts to set goals that describe specific desired changes in participants. We hesitate to anticipate and declare openly ways we hope or need to change.

b. by using as goals *only* short-term task statements.

c. by hurriedly agreeing upon a topic and delegating to the next volunteer leader the job of completing goals and outline.

d. by failing to adjust the topic, goals, and outline when (or if) the volunteer leader is asked to develop them for the group.

e. by becoming hostile because "We spend too much time on mechanics." Sometimes we say, "What we need to do is just go ahead and discuss." And sometimes this is true—particularly when the group is not cohesive enough to tolerate the focusing process. Frequently we must learn through experiencing the inadequate.

f. by losing interest in the whole learning program in order to consciously or unconsciously seek to allay our fears and discomfort.

3. Helping participants focus significant topics.

The following suggestions are specific ways in which trainers can help participants deal with significant topics:

a. The trainer may encourage participants to identify topic areas *after* the group identifies individual problems and needs which they feel they have in common. This suggestion (and the reason for it) can be inserted by the trainer in a brief trainer interruption[5] when the group begins planning its next session.

b. The trainer may encourage the group to set goals which state specific results they hope to attain in their own lives. In an early session, the concept of changing and adjusting goals to fit the developing learning situation can be explained and illustrated in a teaching interlude[6] and in later sessions it can be inserted through trainer interruptions at appropriate times.

c. The trainer may encourage the group to adjust discussion topics and tasks so that they state the intention to deal

[5]See pp. 66-67.
[6]See p. 54.

with the topics in terms of their own feelings, beliefs, and understandings. This procedure has been illustrated as points of focus in above sections. The trainer can illustrate this procedure in an early session and remind the participants through trainer interruptions when they are planning a future session. Several reminders and explanations of this concept will be necessary in early sessions.

d. The trainer may encourage participants to evaluate discussion sessions with great care and honesty during the critique, in terms of stated tasks and goals.

F. Distinguishing Among Topics, Goals, and Tasks

Beginning groups often wonder why their goals are similar to the tasks listed on their outlines. Usually they are listing tasks in both places. In many such cases, the trainer has not yet introduced the idea of goals as desired outcomes which are results of doing tasks. To avoid this the trainer should discriminate between goals and tasks in early sessions and illustrate each.

He should point out as many times as is necessary that, first, the distinction between a task and a goal is an important one, and, next, what the distinction is: that a goal is the end toward which the learning experience is directed, while the task is the specific job that must be tackled in order to reach the goal. The first demonstration discussion, led by the trainer, is a good place to illustrate each by example.

Another misconception is revealed in the question, "Aren't the goal and the topic the same?" This misunderstanding is less likely if the topic is understood as an educational problem in question form and a goal is understood to anticipate a desired change in the learners.

Confusion of goals with topic questions is possible if we consider goals as verbal answers to the topic questions. For example, could the topic "How Can We Improve the Quality of Our Family Life?" be a goal as well as a topic? Obviously not, if goals are seen as changes in people. But if we see goals as end-of-meeting word-packages which answer the question, it is a different matter. If the meeting results in a list of ways to improve family life, has a goal been met? Shouldn't we more properly say that a task has been accomplished? A list of suggested ways of improving family life are words, tentative solutions, to take home from the meeting. We don't know if they are truly ways we can improve our family life until we try them. This is an educational dilemma then: do we aim for a package of information to be taken home from a meeting? Or do we aim for desirable behavior changes resulting from the use of the information by the participants? Obviously, both kinds of result are necessary. But for the sake of simplicity it seems best to think of what we do in the meeting as tasks (making lists, presenting and exploring information, developing solutions, etc.). The human changes that result from what we do at a meeting may thus be thought of as the goals we seek.

Proof that this distinction is desirable comes when we decide to evaluate an educational experience. Do we use goals, or do we use tasks as a yardstick? Is a program successful because meetings end with information which participants agree is interesting and which they can parrot back? Or is a program successful because it helps persons change and behave differently in desirable ways?

The value of achieving tasks during the meetings should not be overlooked, however. Participants get a sense of goal-satisfaction from completing a task, and each such completion usually provides motivation for further activity.

Chapter 4

Conducting the Training Sessions

A. *Introduction*

An agenda for typical training sessions is briefly outlined
below and described in more detail later in this chapter.
Time allotments for each item must be adapted by the
trainer to the demands and needs of the situation—such as
the time available for the session and the stage of development of the group as a team.

B. *The Agenda of a Typical Session*

1. The Trainer's Introduction (Optional: 10 to 20
minutes)

In the early sessions, the trainer should introduce the
purpose of the training, the responsibilities of the participants, the conditions of effective participation, certain group procedures, etc., as needed. This should be
done with care and a kind of pleasant, casual precision.
The beginning of a learning atmosphere should be established. This contact of the trainer with the group is vital
and, when it is concluded, the trainer should have
helped the group to anticipate eagerly the educational
adventure to follow. Each trainer will have a different
way of accomplishing this.

2. Group Discussion (30 minutes to 1½ hours)

Recorder, observer, and discussion leader are selected from participants who volunteer. Discussion is conducted by the group participants. During the discussion the trainer may occasionally intervene (make a trainer interruption), stopping the action momentarily in order to make an observation, raise a question, or give guidance regarding the teamwork process and procedures as it is or should be used by the group. He should not expect much effective participation in the early sessions.

3. Critique

After each discussion, the participants spend from 10 to 20 minutes examining and appraising how they worked together during the discussion. In the early sessions, the trainer usually leads the group during the critique period. Later the critiques begin with the report given by the volunteer observer. Then the group members discuss these observations and, with assistance from the trainer, determine how to improve the learning situation.

4. Planning the Next Session

Before concluding a session, the group plans its next session (10 to 30 minutes). This task usually consists of making four decisions:

a. What topic shall we discuss?

b. What is our tentative goal and how shall we outline it?

c. Who will volunteer to serve as discussion leader and observer?

d. What resources are available to help us prepare for the next session?

C. The First Training Session

The main task at the first session is to initiate the four-step training procedure through an actual discussion experience.[1] The format described here has been used successfully many times.

1. The trainer briefly describes the responsibilities of the discussion leader, group participants, observer, recorder, and resource person. Visual aids (charts or slides) are effective in this presentation.[2] A resourceful trainer can develop his own visual aids. If time allows, a brief review of Chapter 2, Section D would be helpful. These conditions, however, are most meaningful when presented in terms of a live discussion experience.

2. The trainer then assumes the role of discussion leader in order to conduct a demonstration discussion. In many training operations this is the only time he will serve as discussion leader. If a second trainer is available, he can take the role of observer.[3] Next, the trainer-leader helps the group identify an interest-need area and then agree on a topic in that area. Usually there is rapid, but superficial, agreement at this point. After writing up the topic in question form the trainer assists the group to develop at least one goal and an outline. It is important to remember that the trainer is beginning to set a standard in written form by the way he establishes the topic, goals, and outline tasks. As a matter of fact, the trainer is being closely observed by the group participants in everything he does. (See Chapter 3 for guidance in expressing topic, goals, and outline.)

---

[1] In some cases, trainers combine the organizational meeting with the first training session. See Chapter 1 for material on the organizational meeting.

[2] If an organizational meeting preceded the first regular session, Chapter 2 of this book could be assigned at that time as preparation for the first training session. Some trainers may also wish to describe the observer's role at this session.

[3] Some trainers prefer to work together as discussion leader and coleader in this session, with the coleader working as blackboard recorder. In these cases, the role of observer is not introduced until the third or fourth session. It is often an advantage to defer introducing the observer's role in order to reduce initial complexity.

3. The trainer, as leader, conducts the discussion, usually 30 to 45 minutes in length. Some trainers prefer to make the first trainer interruption during this demonstration discussion.

4. The trainer leads the verbal critique of the discussion.[4] If one of the trainers has served as observer, his report should be the first activity in the critique. It should be discussed by the participants, and a checklist of participants' responsibilities[5] used to identify issues which might have been neglected. If an observer's report is not used, the trainer can use a checklist as a guide for conducting the critique.

5. The trainer helps participants prepare for the next session by:

   a. explaining the advantages of having two 30-minute discussions at both the second and the third sessions (see p. 51)
   b. encouraging the group to select topics for the next session
   c. explaining the advantage of using a coleader; asking for and naming the discussion leader(s)
   d. asking for and naming a volunteer observer for the next session *(if one is to be used in the second session)*
   e. suggesting that the participants, *as a group*, develop goals and outlines for the chosen topics, if possible. The alternative is for the volunteer discussion leader(s) to develop suggested goals and outlines to bring to the next session

6. The trainer meets with the volunteer discussion leader(s) between the sessions to inform them on what to expect and to encourage them and give them support.

D. *The Second and Third Sessions*

Both the second and the third training sessions should be 2 to 2½ hours in length. It is helpful if these two sessions

---

[4]Critiques and Trainer Interruptions are described later in this chapter.

[5]A checklist can be made from the participants' responsibilities listed in Chapter 2. See also Appendix B.

are conducted only a few days apart. It is profitable to devote both the second and third training sessions to conducting short discussions, each followed by a critique. Each of these two sessions typically consists of these activities:

▶ a trainer's introduction, reemphasizing the group participants' responsibilities

▶ a 30- to 40-minute discussion under the direction of the volunteer discussion leader(s). The volunteer-observer role is often introduced at the third training session

▶ a 10- to 15-minute critique led by the trainer and introduced by the observer's report, if the role of observer is being used

▶ a second 30- to 40-minute discussion with different volunteer discussion leader(s) and a different observer in their appropriate roles

▶ a second critique led by the trainer

▶ planning the next session—arranging for topics, goals, outlines, discussion leaders, and observers[6]

1. Advantages of Multiple Short Discussions in Early Sessions

a. This procedure employs several participants in the roles of discussion leader and observer in a brief space of time.

b. The typical early topics—broad, impersonal, and pet topics—are rapidly dealt with, and participant-centered topics based on individual needs tend to emerge.

c. Two critiques, rather than one, are held each session. These help build freedom of expression and emphasize the participants' responsibility for the process.

d. The group is given two opportunities each session to learn to manipulate topics, goals, and outlines as means to an end.

---

[6]A short-cut procedure is to choose topics only, letting volunteer discussion leaders submit suggested goals and outlines at the next session. See p. 65 for comments on this procedure.

2. Disadvantages of Short Discussions

a. Participants do not have time, in a 30-minute discussion, to do more than begin to discuss a topic. This is frustrating to some participants who are interested only in the subject content. The trainer can alleviate some of these feelings by alerting participants in advance and by reassuring them that future discussion can deal with the same topics if they desire.

b. Short discussions sometimes bring about an immediate need for information or "answers" in the topic area. The participants may turn to the trainer or to some other resource person and demand an answer. In some cases, the trainers may be tempted to suspend the training session at this point and seize upon this situation as a teachable moment in the area of discussion. To do this may be a mistake.

E. The Trainer as a Guide in Later Sessions

After the early sessions which feature 30- to 45-minute discussions, many training groups adopt a time pattern such as this one for each session:

▶ (Optional, 5-10 minutes) Trainer's carefully prepared remarks

▶ (1 to 1½ hours) Discussion, led by volunteer discussion leader(s) and supported by trainer interruption

▶ (15 to 30 minutes) Critique, conducted by the group, beginning with the volunteer observer's report

▶ (15 to 30 minutes) Planning the next session

Various procedures trainers have used in guiding these four steps are described below.

1. The Trainer's Introduction

A short speech by the trainer (5 to 10 minutes) at the beginning of the session can be used to good advantage, especially during the first four to six sessions.

One effective procedure a trainer can use in his introduction at a given session is to put special emphasis on one or two concepts dealing with process. To follow through on this procedure, the trainer should, during the discussion, (a) make trainer interruptions that illustrate the concepts in operation, and (b) make sure the concepts appear again in the critique. Some concepts to emphasize in a given session are as follows:

a. The leader as an instrument to help the group participants make joint decisions on goals and how to proceed in an attempt to reach them.
b. Communication, what it is and what it requires from participants.
c. A consensus, what it is, why it is used, and when and how it is used.
d. Use of the blackboard as a means to the desired end.
e. Coresponsibility: the participants help each other.
f. The difference between discussion and debate.
g. Goal-setting and the relation of goals to outline-tasks.
h. The need for acceptance and support of some from among participants
i. The significance of listening, of dangling contributions, and of ignored contributions.
j. Doing the task versus personal needs of participants.

The trainer should continue to open each session with a brief introduction as long as it is advisable for effective discussion. Withdrawal of the trainer's introduction can be seen by participants as significant; it signals that the group is becoming more self-sufficient and less dependent upon the trainer.

The trainer has to make delicate decisions as to when a share of the responsibility can be placed on the participants and when to increase it until they are able to take over on their own. When the participants are ready to assume more responsibility, it can be sensed by an adept trainer. Putting them on their own too soon could be so disturbing that the group might be unproductive. On the other hand, keeping them dependent too long could destroy the value of this kind of learning.

"How much is too much?" is a question which perplexes persons in all facets of life. Group participation training is no exception to this problem. By testing now and then, that is, by giving increasing responsibility and seeing how it is accepted, the trainer gets a large part of the answer.

2. The Trainer Interruption

While the group discusses its topic, the trainer has only one tool he can use—the trainer-interruption device. It is a tool which the trainer should explain at the first session, one which gives the trainer authorization to intervene at any time. If it is to be an effective tool, the participants must trust the trainer to use it in their best interests as they function as a developing-learning team. The different kinds of interruption are classified as (a) teaching interludes, (b) observation entries, (c) question entries, and (d) combination entries.

a. The Teaching Interlude. All trainer interruptions are teaching devices of one kind or another to help participants learn to become responsible members of their learning group. But the teaching interlude puts the trainer temporarily in the role of teacher in the traditionally direct sense; that is, of one who explains, illustrates, clarifies, encourages. In this type of trainer interruption, the trainer explains an educational concept, a procedure, or a participant-role responsibility in a talk or short lecture.

The teaching interlude usually requires more time than do the others, and it is used most frequently in the early sessions when the trainer wishes to use the immediacy of a recent group situation to emphasize a basic concept or practice which he is trying to illustrate. Occasionally it is used effectively during the critique period, too, as well as in the midst of the discussion on the chosen topic.

In the early sessions, where this device is most used, the trainer should time these kinds of entries with care. In the early stages, some participants may feel that they haven't dealt enough with the subject (content); thus, the trainer should interrupt with an interlude at some point only when undue frustration is blocking the group or when interaction has already reached a climax and is waning. It is not effective to delay the interruption until interest and involvement are starting to build up to a climax. Identifying these entry points between climaxes in the participants' "satisfaction-cycle" is a skill that the trainer develops through practical experience. This principle of timing applies also to the other types of trainer interruptions.

b. The Observation Entry. This type of trainer interruption is usually a short presentation of data observed and presented for the purpose either of alerting participants to some situation he may wish them to examine together, or of attempting to influence participants' future behavior with respect to some momentary condition that has developed in the group.

The observation entry is usually used after the group has met several times. Like the question entry, it leaves the group free to choose whether to stop and examine their process in view of the trainer's comment or to continue with their discussion.

Observation entries should be brief. They seldom take the form of an observer's report, which usually traces chronologically the events occurring in the group. Instead, the observation entry is often a selective summary of group events designed to present evidence that points to one or two difficulties. It is focusing of observations, phrased so that they reveal the purpose of the observations. For example, a trainer might say:

"At this point, only half of you have contributed to the discussion; this seems to me to be unbalanced participation."

c. The Question Entry. This type of trainer interruption is usually brief, rapierlike. The trainer interrupts, poses a question to call attention to some aspect of the group's procedures or process, and finally indicates that the interruption has ended. The group deals with the question if they wish. This entry is used most frequently in later rather than in early sessions. In early sessions, question entries tend to frustrate participants because they have too little background of experience and principle upon which they can draw to illuminate the significance of the question. The helpful question is based on the trainer's feeling that the participants have the insights necessary to make use of it.

Both the question entry and the observation entry offer opportunities for inadequate trainers to confuse a group in the early stages. The poorly informed trainer may raise obscure, sometimes even pedantic, questions or observations, with a sort of triumphant, cryptic defiance, as if to say:

"See how much I know of this highly technical secret stuff? See if you can figure out what I have said. I dare you to! You've got to dig this out the hard way."

The intent of the question entry is usually (a) to provide an opportunity for participants to examine without further trainer assistance how they carried on during a recent group event or situation, or (b) to encourage individual thinking on some process or procedure problem that might lead to more effective discussion without involving the participants in group appraisal.

If the trainer is not careful he will be pushed by the group participants into answering the question himself. Since participants in the early sessions are somewhat dependent, they often seek to turn the question entry into a teaching interlude to escape dealing with the problem themselves. Later, as independence develops, they may seem to ignore the question entry entirely.

d. The Combination Entry. The combination entry is a trainer interruption in which the trainer uses some combination of trainer observations, questions, and teaching interludes. Usually responses of participants are called for following this kind of interruption—the one most often used by trainers in the early sessions. It may be used to some extent throughout all the sessions, but if the group members learn to use volunteer observers effectively, the trainer has less need to use interruptions of any kind in later sessions.

In the early sessions, participants need to respond to trainer observations and questions. Also, they need to have their responses guided toward the expression of their feelings about the situation, and toward discovering why an event occurred or why a certain procedure is significant. For these reasons the combination entry is very useful, and usually falls into patterns such as these:

▶ —observation plus brief commentary on significance (trainer)

  —responses (participants and trainer)

▶ —observation plus question (trainer)

  —responses (participants and trainer)

▶ —observation plus brief commentary (trainer)

  —responses (participants)

  —teaching interlude

  —responses (trainer and participants)

▶ —observation (trainer)

  —teaching interlude (trainer)

  —responses (participants and trainer)

3. The Language and Manner of the Trainer

The way in which the trainer describes events in the group will affect the emotional climate, which in turn will have a lot to do with the way adults learn and what they learn. Particularly is this true during trainer-interruptions and critiques. It is most desirable for the trainer to use emotionally neutral words in describing group events. This does not mean that he should avoid being animated and enthusiastic; he must be specific and as accurate as possible about what has happened and not sugarcoat it.

One danger to avoid is that of using emotionally charged terminology or jargon in an attempt to intensify and accelerate the training experience beyond its natural pace. Jargon should be avoided. It irritates many literate people and is likely to intimidate some persons because of its unfamiliarity.

Metaphors which are too closely associated with death, suffering, and violence should not be used to achieve emphasis. They can produce a false intensity that defeats the training process. Some examples are:

▶ "Suffering death"—being ignored or not listened to, feeling rejected.

▶ "Being clobbered"—being verbally attacked.

▶ "Committing murder"—cutting off someone's contribution, attacking someone verbally, ignoring someone else's contribution.

▶ "Crying out"—indications that a participant needs help in order to participate more fully.

▶ "Being crucified"—being a scapegoat; also similar to 1 and 2 above.

▶ "Taking off the masks"—saying what we really think and feel.

▶ "Being resurrected"—being accepted, listened to, and brought back into active participation after having been "killed" or "maimed" by some means listed above.

This group-participation-training experience is a significantly new idea in itself to most learners. It should be remembered that the learner in this adventure is trying to cope with the problem of changing learning habits which may be deeply engrained. He has been taught in the past to memorize and repeat his memorizations. He who could memorize the most and the fastest and report it correctly was rewarded one way or another. The fellow learner didn't count for much in the total learning experience. Now, the learner is asked to consider his fellows' motives, to help his fellow learners learn, and to assume a great share of the whole learning procedure —learning to be responsible by accepting responsibility, and learning how to study seriously what the subject under consideration means to him.

These ideas cause enough frustration without adding a new language. Good straightforward English is adequate to the task and it is strongly recommended that trainers use it.

4. Some Principles of Trainer Interruption

a. The trainer-interruption technique should be introduced to the group at the first training session. The trainer should explain what it is during his introductory remarks and then make one or two brief interruptions in the first discussion in order to demonstrate the technique.

b. More interruptions by the trainer should take place in the beginning sessions than in the later ones. At the start, participants usually need more support than they do later, in order to maintain optimum structure and motivation. Frequent appropriate interruptions in the early sessions are valuable; the trainer can use them to point out factors which are embarrassing for a beginning group to identify. Thus, the trainer can help establish an atmosphere conducive to freedom of expression in the early sessions.

c. The trainer should avoid shocking the participants or adding to the hostility inherent in a situation by analyzing fundamental conflicts.

d. Motives or causes of behavior beyond the immediate group situation should not be pursued, either in interruptions or in critiques.

e. The interruption should be used to support a victim of poor group teamwork.

f. The leader should avoid giving long technical interpretations. These promote dependency on the trainer as one who can always be relied upon to make expert diagnoses.

g. Interruptions should not be made:
to contribute to the content area of the discussion; to comment unfavorably on the performance of individual participants; to correct participants' ideas about the topic; or to interpret content resource materials for the group. This can be done more safely in later sessions.

h. Interruptions should be timed to relieve excessive frustration; to interfere least with the satisfaction expected when participants discuss a topic or subject; and to promote understanding of effective process and procedure.

F. The Critique

The critique is conducted immediately after each discussion has ended. It is a verbal appraisal of the discussion experience. Shared by all participants, it is a period of usually 10 to 20 minutes during which the participants identify and discuss the obstacles encountered and the successful accomplishments in their discussion teamwork and individual learning for the purpose of improving future learning experiences.

In order to describe procedures used in critiques, the trainer's function, and points of trainer withdrawal, the critique is here broken down into three parts.

1. Introducing the Critique.

The trainer's introduction to the critique aims to prepare the participants to share actively in it. It is a brief transitional period designed to tell the purpose of the critique and how it will be conducted; and to remind all members of the group to participate freely.

In the early sessions the trainer leads the critique in order to demonstrate how to do it, and to continue to encourage the participants to examine their accomplishments carefully. As soon as some feeling of freedom has developed and the participants have begun to accept the procedure of openly assessing their teamwork in the learning adventure, the trainer begins withdrawing his active leadership of the critique. Usually, he encourages the volunteer discussion leader, with the help of the observer, to assume nominal leadership. The trainer thus gives up his temporary job of introducing and leading the critique. Giving up this function is significant as one of the points of withdrawal for the trainer.

2. Conducting the Critique.

Most groups eventually use both of the two following critique methods:

This method is often used during the first two to four sessions, before the role of observer is introduced and filled by volunteers. The trainer and each participant has a checklist of participants' responsibilities.[7] The trainer conducts the early critiques by leading participants from item to item on the checklist, asking appropriate questions about the performance of the group and encouraging the participants to express their feelings and opinions.

In early critiques, the trainer can interpret helpfully and enlarge upon the checklist as he conducts the critique. Many observations and questions can be introduced regarding the checklist items. Often the trainer finds it useful to insert questions such as these to identify feelings and events that occurred during the discussion:

Did anyone say something he feels was not understood?

Did anyone make a contribution that was overlooked?

Did anyone have something appropriate to say, but could not find the opportunity to say it?

If any participants respond positively (verbally or by gestures) to such questions, the trainer immediately knows he has located a possible leverage point which he can use to help the participants deal with their own experience. He has only to follow up with questions that probe how, when, and why it happened.

During the early critiques, the trainer can expect the participants to make superficial comments about learning activities. There will be a natural reluctance to express true feelings. It usually does more harm than good for the trainer to try to accelerate the development of free expression by pleading. It is far better for him to express some critique observations on his own per-

---

[7]This may be constructed from lists found in Chapter 2.

formance or on their teamwork in order to set a standard, as for instance:

"I noticed that several contributions were apparently not heard during the discussion. Some were not acknowledged and others ignored. How do you account for this? Whose responsibility was it?"

The critique begins with an observer's report. Next, the group discusses these observations. Finally, a checklist of participant responsibilities is used to make sure that neglected aspects of the process are discussed.

In the early critiques, participants frequently create two problems for the trainer. One stems from their request to the trainer, "Tell us what we should have done." The second problem arises from the defensive conclusion: "That observer's report is wrong." Both of these situations should lead to answers which participants must learn to provide with the trainer's help.

There is a danger here that the trainer will not appraise this situation shrewdly. He may try to answer their questions, or he may give them a charitable smile, say nothing, and increase the learner's frustration beyond the point where productive learning can take place. The trainer has to see to it that problems and questions which arise are answered. It is in the way they are answered, and by whom, that the significance lies.

If, after giving the group every opportunity to come to some reasonable and helpful answer to a question, they still fail to arrive at a solution solid enough that it would supply a support for future parts of this learning process, the trainer has several alternatives. He can suggest that the group get at the answers by finding a resource person who knows, or he can assign two or three members of the group the responsibility of finding the answer in the library or any place else they can find it. Or he may ask leading questions which give the participants clues and so lead them to find their own answers.

There is danger in putting a group so much on its own that they don't know what they are doing or what's being done with them. A skilled trainer, like a skilled leader, knows when to move in and when to move out, when to be relaxed and when to put on the pressure.

3. Terminating the Critique

After the participants have expressed themselves in the critique proper, trainers may find it useful in early sessions to add a brief teaching interlude. This is the trainer's opportunity to comment upon factors of the discussion teamwork not covered in the critique. The trainer sometimes uses this form of verbal participation in the later sessions after he has withdrawn from active participation during the first parts of the sessions. In these terminal remarks he can present points which will serve as notice of his recognition of the group's maturation.

Some trainers terminate the critique period by asking one or more questions designed to extend the freedom of expression that has developed. Trainers have used questions such as those that follow to give participants an opportunity to summarize and personalize the appraisal of the process:

"If you had this session to do over, what would you do differently

   —as individual participants?"

   —as a group?"

"Did anyone change his idea of another participant as a result of this session?" (Don't press by asking "Whose?" or "In what way?" Let any answer be a voluntary response. If someone responds, but apparently does not wish to explain himself fully, the trainer can remind the group that participation is voluntary.)

4. Bad-Good Behavior in the Group

Role responsibilities for group participants and discussion leaders are given in the first sessions. The suggestions here are not to be interpreted as absolute standards which could be used to make judgments about "bad" and "good" behavior in the group. Few could prescribe behavior that would fit all discussion situations at all times and, therefore, none should be treated as absolute standards.

What happens in a group is not of itself "bad" or "good" but a symptom of some factor that helps or hinders effective learning and group functioning. For example, every fringe conversation that occurs during a discussion is not by definition "bad." It may fill a need and may indicate high motivation. Whether it disrupted communication and had an effect on the discussion, in a given case, and why, can be explored by the participants. Participants need to find out why things happen in their groups and what is their effect, rather than waste their time sitting in judgment upon each other.

5. A Summary of Critique Essentials for Trainers

a. The trainer should get participants involved responsibly in critiques as soon as possible.

b. He should emphasize the responsibility of all participants for the success of discussion teamwork. Individuals may need to be protected from being made scapegoats for ineffective teamwork.

c. Participants should be given a chance to learn how to help each other find the answers to some of their questions. The trainer will help them learn to do this rather than answer their questions. He will cite general principles, but will not tell them exactly what to feel, think, or do. He will encourage them to express how they feel about the teamwork in their discussion, what they think the obstacles were, and how they can improve their total participation.

G. Planning the Next Session

After the discussion critique, the group has one final task—to plan the next session. In the early sessions, until a standard procedure has been established, the trainer usually leads the group in this task.

There are several approaches which might be used to plan the next session. Two examples are given here.

APPROACH I

In one approach the group chooses the topic; the volunteer discussion leaders and observer are secured; and the volunteer discussion leaders are asked to prepare an outline and suggested goals to submit to the group at the beginning of the next session. This idea seems to save time because it allows the training session to move to a rapid conclusion.

This approach has been used successfully by many training groups.

APPROACH II

In another approach, the participants as a group choose the next topic; set tentative goals; construct a tentative discussion outline; and focus these elements into a unit. Volunteer discussion leaders and an observer are then secured. Although more time is needed for the use of this procedure, it seems highly advantageous for several reasons:

▶ shared planning increases feelings of joint responsibility and ego involvement and is an added opportunity to practice the discussion teamwork process during the planning itself.

► conditions develop in which participants are most likely to volunteer as discussion leaders.

► participants will feel freer to adjust the goals and outline to their needs at the beginning of the next meeting.

► this approach takes immediate advantage of the understanding and freedom of expression that has developed in the discussion and in the verbal critique; thus, topic selection is often more personalized.

► it provides some definite guideposts for between-meeting preparation by participants.

Regardless of which of these two approaches is used in planning the next session, it is desirable for the group to choose the topic (or the topic, goal, and outline) before volunteers are sought for the roles of discussion leader and observer. Participants volunteer to serve more readily in situations that are known and defined in advance. Also they are most likely to volunteer for discussion leader:

► when they can work as coleader with another participant;

► if the trainer reminds the participants that the discussion leader is no more responsible for the success of the discussion than are the group participants and that the discussion leader does not have to be an expert in the topic area; or

► if the trainer offers to consult with the volunteer discussion leaders before the next session.

Since the trainer leads the end-of-session planning in early sessions, he is at that time in a good position to give guidance in program planning, toward: selecting a topic based on interests and needs, setting goals, developing an outline, and focusing[8] the topic by bringing the first three elements into adjustment. The trainer must be careful not

---

[8]For the focusing process, see the appropriate section in Chapter 3.

to suggest topics, goals, or outline tasks. He can, however, help participants cast their suggestions in an effective visible form.[9] And he can explain the relationship between these elements as he helps the participants in their planning. Usually the trainer is able to withdraw his active leadership in the planning after a few sessions, leaving this function to the volunteer discussion leader so that the group can begin to function as a self-sufficient unit. His withdrawal from this function is significant; it helps the participants begin to recognize their growing independence.

Planning the next session often includes identifying informational resources which participants can use to prepare for the next session. This is especially important after the group has progressed beyond short, 30-minute discussions. Films and role-playing can be used appropriately as sources of information and for presenting opinions and reactions, as long as they do not overshadow or replace the training process. Most training groups usually fall back on written materials and resource persons. Often the trainer must call to the group's attention the possibility of broadening the fund of resources with charts, graphs, maps, slides, films, and appropriate educational procedures.

The resource person, when one is used, should not be asked to start the meeting. The participants' goals, outline, and their discussion must not become subordinate to the resource person's speech. The resource person should fit into the group operation as a repository of information to be used as needed during the discussion.

H. Accomplishing Withdrawal

Trainers should withdraw their initial leadership as participants become responsible. They encourage this assumption of responsibility in the following ways:

---

[9]See Chapter 3, Section D for suggested illustrations.

▶ The trainer's introduction at the start of the sessions is omitted when its use seems unnecessary.

▶ Trainer interruptions during the discussion are reduced in quantity as the need diminishes.

▶ The trainer's introduction to, and leadership of, the critique is turned over at the appropriate time to the volunteer discussion leader and the observer.

▶ The trainer's terminal remarks in the critique are reduced in quantity and can finally be omitted.

▶ The trainer's guidance in planning the next session is released to the volunteer discussion leader. He reduces guidance to occasional assistance from outside the group, and finally tries to omit his part entirely.

The trainer's role is to withdraw gradually and turn the responsibility for the whole learning operation over to the participants. Care must be exercised that he does not withdraw too soon, or hold on too long.

I. Stages of Development in the Group

The participants in a training group seem to develop, as a group, through three characteristic stages. The characteristics describing these stages do not apply to all participants in a group, but are general tendencies and concepts that seem to account for these tendencies.

STAGE I: DEPENDENCE. Everyone is in some degree immature. In varying degrees individuals depend upon people's opinion of them for their sense of security. This is a natural and healthy reaction, but when overdone becomes harmful. In a new group, most people fear to express their real feelings and opinions until they know it is safe. To express their differences—to act independently—is to risk appearing different from the others and, thus, to risk losing the approval they need. In the early sessions, therefore, many participants express themselves in clichés and superficial talk. The boundaries of what they can say and do in the group, and still feel accepted as like the others, are not yet defined. Most of them have been trained in home, church, and school to be passive participants. They follow established rules and speak of their concurrence with approved ideas. The contribution which they might make takes a kind of courage that has been trained out of many persons in today's society.

Usually participants do not expose their individual learning problems in this stage; they will not disagree vigorously on issues they discuss. Topics they agree to discuss are fairly safe topics or are kept safe. Most training groups begin to develop beyond this sort of probing stage in from two to six sessions.

The value that results from each person's feeling that he is at least partly responsible for the success of this type of learning experience cannot be underestimated. The trainer and discussion leader and group participants must help each other express opinions and ideas for what they are worth without having such an emotional investment in them that they get upset if the ideas are altered or rejected.

A training group starts with conformity. It proceeds to release some individualism (stage II), and finally, it renders freedom productive through the development of individual discipline and interpersonal responsibility (stage III).

STAGE II: COMPETITIVE INDEPENDENCE. Man feels frustrated if he throttles the expression of his unique individual experiences and opinions too long. He wants to express his true self (his differences from the others) as well as to be accepted as a member of the group. These two contradictory needs are a basic ambivalence: dependence—independence. Man is both gregarious and autonomous. Conflicting opinions emerge and bring threats of change which man sometimes does not wish to accept. Participants naturally tend to defend themselves against ideas which seem to threaten them—ideas which raise the possibility of their having to change present attitudes and beliefs.[11] They try to prove that their opinions are right and others' are wrong. Few attempt to find out why others feel and believe as they do. Some participants make active attempts to change other participants' views, usually through logic or persuasion or force of argument. There is both attack and defense, characterized by much telling and little asking. Sometimes there is much haggling over definitions and a search for absolute meanings. Frequently, participants cite opinions of authorities, persons, books (even page references), to do battle for them.

Some persons feel that independence means developing their own ideas or having their own way, at the expense of others if necessary. Those who can talk the longest and loudest will continue to the point where they make nuisances of themselves in order to establish a kind of pecking order. This kind of participant feels more comfortable in a social situation where there are clear-cut bosses and those who know their places. He will strive to maintain or to re-establish an atmosphere which closely resembles one in which he has been trained. The authoritarian environment with which he is familiar may not be satisfactory, but it is more satisfactory than one which threatens change.

Everyone feels this frustration to some degree, but some much more than others. Actually, part of this confusion, which greatly affects the way one learns, is bound up with the problem of discipline. We seem to like a neat system whereby we have the disciplinarian and the disciplined. While this may not be completely satisfactory, we mistakenly feel that it is one way to temporarily dispose of the pressing problem of self-discipline.

---

[11]One or more of three methods of defense may appear as: physical withdrawal (nonattendance), silence during discussion, often characterized by physical gestures representing dissatisfaction or anger, and verbal attack.

This is where quality leadership comes in and freedom of expression begins to develop, if the meetings are carefully handled by the trainer and later by the discussion leader. Participation in this stage of competitive independence continues to be somewhat ego-centered, as individual participants begin to assert their unique individual differences and to defend themselves against change, but they are not so restrained as previously by their need for approval by the other group members.

STAGE III: COOPERATIVE INDEPENDENCE (INTERDEPENDENCE). As participants move on to this point in their development, they feel freer to say what they mean because they know that other participants are more likely to accept them as they are. No longer do they attack each other with vehemence or try to change each other. They might disagree, but they see each other as persons with feelings and ideas instead of as opponents against whom they must defend themselves. They are interested in why each believes as he does. They try actively to understand each other so they can help each other struggle with his own learning problem. Freed from feeling the necessity of defending themselves against others, and from the need to appear all-competent and all-knowing, participants find they can learn together productively, even though learning is essentially an individual matter.

J. Perspectives

Trainers and participants usually work together during several of the sessions with different perspectives of time and intent. The trainer sees developments in the group in terms of how they fit into a pattern of productive development over a period of time. He sees events in the light of both past occurrences and desired future outcomes. The participants, on the other hand, do not take a long-term view of the teamwork process development. They are caught

71

up in the living present of each session. They are concerned with themselves and with what now is. The satisfactions sought by participants in Stages I and II are immediate and personal, largely in terms of meeting individual needs for approval and for resisting change. Since the training goals are not well understood during the first few sessions, participants do not understand the significance of development until after some of it has occurred, over a period of time, and been identified in behavioral terms during the critiques.

Stated discussion goals pursued by group participants are concerned mainly with increased understandings of the content material or topic. The trainer, in contrast, is concerned with helping participants change their attitudes and behaviors toward each other as colearners and toward the process of working together. He is concerned with relationships of people because he knows that this is vital if learning is to be integrated and productive. Group participants are preoccupied with themselves, mainly "me," and subject-matter relationships—at least on the conscious level.

For many sessions, participants may discuss problems that lie outside themselves and the group—problems related to an organization, a community, or the world at large. They look outward for topics and away from personal threats. Trainers try to direct attention inward, toward the learning problems common to the participants and toward the resources of the individual learners and the group.

Participants frequently see written resource materials as ends in themselves—items to be understood through discussion. The trainer sees all materials as means to an end, and he thinks of the learning tasks as being most properly set by participants, not by resource materials. To reconcile these two sets of perspectives the effective trainer does not attempt to impose his own views by force of logic. He must bide his time and help the participants discover together in the training experience the effective principles of learning.

Chapter 5

Some Common Problems in Training Sessions

Certain misunderstandings and problems are likely to occur in any social situation. In participation training, these problems appear more frequently during the early sessions. Suggestions for their solution are given here, both for trainers and for other participants, but these suggestions should not be considered as the only courses of action or the only possible explanations.

A. *Distinguishing between the Discussion Leader and the Trainer*

The discussion leader is a participant who volunteers to direct the group in the discussion of a topic. The trainer gives leadership, too, but he does not lead the group in discussing its topic. He exerts leadership in a different way—by helping participants learn effective processes and procedures and improve their discussion teamwork. It is important that participants recognize this distinction.

B. *Overconcern for Satisfaction with the Discussion of the Topic*

This problem can be restated as inadequate concern by participants for developing (and learning about) effective

73

working relationships in the group. Participants' initial concern is for immediate subject satisfaction, immediate completion of what they consider the educational task. And to many participants the educational task is simply to cover the lesson or topic, to hear information given or the answer revealed.

Most people, when they are involved in learning experiences, don't think as much about people as they do about subjects. They must recognize that in this type of training people, not subjects, are taught. Until they come to understand this concept, they are likely to become involved in exercises in pedantry rather than in creative learning experiences.

When participants find that they are expected to spend some of their time in each session learning to work together so they can eventually explore content (subjects) more meaningfully, and that they cannot learn to work effectively together immediately, they begin to search for the causes of their lack of understanding. Seldom do they point to themselves. Instead, they tend to blame the trainer or something external, such as structural elements of the situation. They may also express their frustrations by becoming impatient with recording on the board, with carefully wording the topic, setting goals, adjusting the outline—and getting group consensus on these matters.

Early feelings of frustration often reveal that participants have not yet fully understood and/or accepted the goals of participation training. These impatient participants still have an image of education as the receiving of information or answers from somebody else. In their drive to cover the topic, they forget the training goals: learning more about themselves as learners, how they relate to others, how they can help others, and the dynamics of the learning situation and how it can be made more effective. They do not yet recognize these kinds of learning as educational. Nor do they think of this learning process as an active search for personal meaning, with subjects contributing, not dominating, factors in this adventure.

The participants' drive for satisfaction on a subject level is an important motivation factor in early sessions, and it must not be denied by the actions or inaction of the trainer. One of his main jobs is to help the participants become aware of their relationships to each other through the processes of participation training. This is best accomplished if the participants gain content or subject satisfaction while they learn about processes and procedures.

C. Time Spent on Adjusting Topic, Goals, and Outline

The trainer may frustrate the participants unduly by denying them enough content satisfaction in the early stage. If, at the start, the trainer overemphasizes process and procedures and insists that they choose a deeply personal topic, that the goals be extremely specific and personal, and that the group spend a major portion of the time focusing topic, goals, and outline, the beginning group may tend to spin its wheels and never get to the discussion itself. Participants will then protest, with some justification, that too much time is being spent on "mechanics."

Trainers tend to err in one of three ways in this situation: by making too few trainer-interruptions, by making too many trainer-interruptions, or by putting too much (or too little) pressure on the group participants to get at the important aspects of this learning job.

If the trainer passively sits by and offers little or no assistance with topic, goals, and outline, the group will accuse him of withholding assistance. Some trainers wrongly assume that everything must be learned by self-discovery. This is as much in error as the other extreme, namely, that everybody who studies enough subjects will be educated.

If the trainer makes frequent lengthy interruptions, the participants are overwhelmed by complexity as well as dismayed by the fact that they are not learning enough information about their topic. He wrongly assumes that participants will discover very little from experience (by analyzing it later in the critique) and that the trainer must explain every detail whenever an opportunity arises. The trainer wastes time if he *insists* that participants learn about process and procedure before any discussion of the subject can take place. There must be discussion involving content in order to teach process and procedure.

A balanced approach is necessary. If some participants do not grasp the concept of goal and outline *via* trainer-interruptions early in a session, perhaps they will understand it an hour later when the discussion experience is analyzed in the critique; if not then, perhaps three sessions later. The trainer cannot dictate when and how learning must take place.

D. Choosing Topics Too Broad in Scope

This results in an inability to focus the topic on individual problems and needs common to the experience of the participants which they think they can do something about. See "Focusing the Topic," Chapter 3, for suggestions.

E. Thinking of the Training Group as a Social Action Group

A training group usually is not organized to initiate social action or to start projects. It is ideally a learning group that eventually should deal with individual needs and learning problems common to the participants. Topics discussed in the early phase are often concerned with the organizational difficulties and community problems. Discussing these problems seems naturally to move participants toward doing something about them. If the training group is to accomplish its basic purposes, participants should hold in check this desire for immediate concerted action. After the training group has achieved its training goals, it can proceed more fruitfully to take action, if participants so desire.

Participants push for social action in the beginning partly because they cannot freely discuss subjective or personal problems. As sessions progress, topics tend to evolve from general, nonpersonal problems toward the specific and the personal. Thus, beginning groups usually choose topics involving world, state, community, or organizational problems. Several sessions pass, usually, before individual problems and needs common to the participants emerge and are brought into topical focus. Some groups actually begin by discussing some aspect of outer space. This is about as far as they can flee from their individual learning problems.

This does not mean that a training group must never discuss such topics as "Should this community (or organization) sponsor a youth center?" or "Why has our Church attendance fallen off?" These topics may be the basis on which the participants are willing to start. After all, they must accept the responsibility for choosing their own topics. But, since the training group is primarily a learning group, it is not organized to make group decisions on problems of social action.

7. Decisions by Consensus

Since a training group is primarily a learning group, not an action group, it does not make group decisions to be implemented through activities beyond the group. Participants in a training group need to make group decisions only about their own procedures, topics, goals, and outlines. In other words, the training group is a decision-making group only when it is planning some aspect of its own learning activity. On these matters, it is desirable for participants to reach some consensus of opinion.

As the word "consensus" is used here, it is meant to convey the idea of a kind of general, tentative agreement. Consensus in group participation is reached when participants have an opportunity to discuss and explore a problem and then, on the basis of their deliberations, come to some tentative, working agreement. This provisional agreement is the result of concessions made from both minority and majority views.

Consensus rarely results in an agreement with which everyone is completely happy, but it is a good enough compromise with which to move along for a while, until participants wish to take another look at the problem in the light of changes which may have taken place as the group learned more about the problem.

Consensus involves both unanimity and disagreement. Using consensus to reach group decisions is significant because it gives every participant an opportunity to express himself and thereby take part in the group's decision and yet the participant may openly maintain some reservations. It is worth remembering that the way decisions are made can affect the quality and quantity of participation, and the nature of what is learned. Sometimes it even determines who will attend the next session.

G. Taking a Vote

From the start, the participants must make decisions in selecting topics, setting goals, developing the outline (tasks), and determining procedures. It is desirable for these decisions to be made by consensus. Often, however, in early sessions, participants wish to resort to voting as a quick way to make decisions. This desire usually springs from one or more of these reasons:

> Some participants are accustomed to resolving conflicts by voting and don't yet understand the significance of trying to reach consensus. They tend to be interested only in the content of the discussions; they do not see planning together as a potential learning experience in itself, as an opportunity not only to help others, but also to help ourselves understand why we are reacting as we are.

In this kind of activity, they can learn more about themselves and how they can make their individual contribution and, at the same time, learn about other persons and how to work with them. They are fatigued and do not have the patience to try to reach consensus.

They think they are right and refuse to give a little in order to reach a working agreement.

When participants wish to take a vote, it is often productive for the trainer to ask the participants, first, if they understand what consensus is. If they do not, perhaps they should hear about it. Second, the trainer can ask if they wish to explore why they wish to vote, and the advantages and disadvantages they recognize in voting. Voting saves time and gets decisions made. But it also often sets up a militant minority which sometimes becomes a nuisance and slows down the progress of the group.

H. Belief that Tasks and Goals Need Not Be Written and Agreed On

Shared tasks and goals are required if participants are to work toward the same educational end. Making the tasks and goals visible on a blackboard helps ensure that at least they are known to all present. At each session, knowing what they propose to do together and why they propose to do it is important. Learning to make these decisions together is part of the training procedure. Many participants try to avoid agreeing on tasks and goals by saying, "We all know why we are here, so why should we write it down? Besides, if we carefully work out our tasks and goals in advance, we shall be robbing ourselves of creativity. We shall be fenced in later by decisions we make now. Let's just let the discussion develop where it will."

Agreement by participants on discussion tasks and goals is helpful, even though a tentative agreement, or consensus, is reached only one session in advance. It gives direction to the preparation accomplished between meetings. Also, it sensitizes participants to the need for a goal on which they can agree and is especially useful when the group evaluates its achievements. Finally, tasks and goals are not at all unchangeable after they have been formulated. The participants can change them any time they have good reason and agree to do so. Learning to make necessary changes together is part of the training.

I. Setting Goals that Are Vague and Impersonal

Since topics in the early sessions tend to be broad and impersonal, the tasks and goals will probably reflect this tendency. Goals become more specific and personally meaningful and attainable when they are based on identifiable problems and needs common to the participants. (See "Focusing the Topic," Chapter 3.)

J. Tendency to Discuss Topics in Impersonal Abstract Terms

In most beginning groups, participants avoid revealing their true feelings and understandings about the topic under discussion. Until the individuality of each participant has been rewarded by acceptance from the other participants, feelings and personal opinions will tend to be expressed guardedly. Slowly, usually, they emerge as participants learn that they can trust each other and that they will be heard. Until freedom of expression develops, most groups use a host of devices to avoid pursuing topics that might be fruitfully personalized. Some of these are:

1. Resistance to focusing the discussion so that tasks and goals will apply to the individual members of the group and to their experiences. ("Let's quit fooling with tasks and goals and get into the discussion.")
2. Compiling lists of problems, advantages, attributes, solutions, etc., with little attention to implications

3. Speculating on what might be, rather than exploring what is.
4. Discussing academically the abstract meaning of certain passages in a resource book as an end in itself, rather than using these resources as means of understanding and solving individual problems and needs common to the participants.
5. Hair-splitting and attempting to formulate absolute definitions of words rather than exploring what participants personally believe and understand.
6. Making fun, either overtly or subtly, of those group participants who try to get the problem into the concrete from the abstract. Sometimes an abstractionist will try to draw others into fruitless disputation partly to show off and partly to keep from getting at the real problem.

K. Administrator's Expectations of Smooth, Satisfying Discussions at the Start

Because participants are learning to become jointly responsible for the learning experience, the early sessions will not be fully satisfying as subject-matter learning experiences. This fumbling is the price we pay when we are exposed to new experiences.

Some administrators and teachers might say, "My people deserve the best; therefore, I or some other subject expert will lead the discussion." These persons' ideas of what is best for learners are often based on their interest in (1) immediately getting content they think people need presented to participants, (2) covering a topic as they think it should be covered, (3) covering a certain prescribed lesson on time, (4) getting certain "truths" across to the participants, or (5) preventing wrong ideas from being stated by participants. These kinds of persons are likely to become disturbed during early sessions. They cannot appreciate the use of discussion except as a direct teaching method.

L. The Pooling of Ignorance

Some persons believe it is a waste of time for adults to sit together in groups and express opinions that are not based on known facts, or are at variance with known facts. These persons usually believe that the facts (as *they* understand them) are of supreme importance, that what learners think and feel is not so important, and that people who do not know the facts are wasting time by talking "off the top of their heads." Because of this attitude, participants hesitate to reveal their ignorance because someone with the facts will immediately set them straight. This situation leaves little room for personal exploration by the group participants.

It cannot be denied that facts are necessary for productive discussion. But it is also appropriate and essential to productive group learning for adults to express conceptions they happen to cherish. They have a stake in their beliefs. The educational process is emotional as well as intellectual, and personal prejudices must be taken into consideration.

Improper use of group-participation training can frustrate and befuddle the participants just as the misuse of anything can cause trouble. Untrained or poorly trained discussion leaders, who want to do well and may be quite sincere about it, have frequently failed to accomplish anything worthwhile by trying to use the procedure advocated here. This kind of educational activity can be suited to adult academic training with great profit if it is conducted by skilled personnel. Untrained leaders who allow an unprepared group to sit around a table and aimlessly talk could be responsible for wasting time through pooling ignorance.

Those who understand learning as something more than the accumulation of facts help others become more understanding of the relationships which exist between facts and their personal development. Theirs is a refreshing approach providing rewards not found in the torpid system of learning which encourages the parroting of ideas. They can assist persons to learn to interpret what they hear and see and read. They can help people understand that new ideas count for something and are not "things" which must be fitted into a highly efficient, mechanical education factory. They can help all kinds of persons explore their potentials and learn to express themselves in some satisfying and creative enterprise that can contribute to their social and personal growth.

Good trainers and discussion leaders can help themselves and the other participants match a system of learning experiences with what we claim to be the kind of social and spiritual life we have or desire to have. By properly using the educational insights incorporated in group participation training, all participants should be able to learn more about self-discipline and use it more efficiently to further the intensity and scope of their learning about people and things.

M. Extremes of Participation

In the early stages, volunteer discussion leaders and group participants often tend toward several extremes. Either they take a very active part and dominate the discussion, or else they do very little to help the group.

1. *The dominating discussion leader* is often trying to use group discussion as a direct teaching method. He has information or preconceived ideas about the topic and he tries to persuade the group participants to accept his ideas. Some signs of this kind of leadership are evident:

▶ when a discussion leader keeps discussion proceeding along certain avenues without inquiring into the feelings of the other participants. He overlooks or ignores many of the contributions, or disposes of them arbitrarily; he puts the group back on the track he has chosen without asking whether the group would like to examine its position and make changes or adjustments.

- when a discussion leader rewords contributions to make them fit his outline, his preferred conclusion, or point them toward the particular "truth" he is trying to emphasize.

- when a discussion leader initiates questions rapidly in an attempt to secure the answer he seeks. He does not help the group explore the significance of the answers he rejects, but quickly asks other questions.

- when a discussion leader will not deviate from the outline he has submitted, but defends it aggressively as the best approach to the topic. This is one reason why it is often best for the group as a whole to plan the next session at the conclusion of each meeting. Such an important step should not be left to one person, even if he volunteers to do the job.

- when a discussion leader abandons his neutrality and becomes teacher and information-giver. Neutrality of the discussion leader, of course, is less important after the group participants have developed freedom and responsibility.

- when a discussion leader openly judges the worth of participants' contributions by praising some and overlooking or frowning upon others.

The dominating discussion leader, like the unqualified teacher, often uses fear as his ally. The kind of adult learning predicated on fear is indeed lasting and effective. The reservoir of untapped human resources that have been kept in check through overtly or subtly using fear as a learning aid is staggering. The number of us who have been taught to be immature by parents, churches, and schools is not too difficult to discern if we examine how we use our learning, how we relate to each other, and the manner in which we operate most of our social institutions.

2. *The inactive discussion leader* gives the group participants little help in determining their direction and procedure. Often he is afraid to make a move for fear

of being judged undemocratic or authoritarian. In early sessions this kind of discussion leader sometimes frustrates the group participants because they still long for the strong, directive out-in-front type of leadership to which they have been accustomed in learning groups. Since the group participants do not yet actively exercise their responsibilities for moving the group forward, a leadership vacuum results for the first few minutes. Then the following signs are likely to appear:

▶ A "strong" group participant, or a clique of two or three like-minded group participants, will fill the discussion leadership vacuum and start things going, usually without regard for consensus on the task.

▶ Much telling and little asking will be evidenced in the discussion.

▶ Active participants will tend to forget the teamwork process and to devote their full attention to content.

▶ Few attempts will be made to understand the significance and meaning of the participants' contributions; few attempts to build on each other's contributions; contributions will be left dangling, unacknowledged; few attempts will be made to draw contributions from the group participants who do not take part spontaneously.

3. *The dominating group participant.* Many training groups have one or more participants who talk so much that they exhaust the patience and discourage the active participation of others. Usually, these persons do more telling than asking, that is, they make few attempts to understand contributions of others or to draw others into the discussion. Their contributions tend to be self-centered statements of what they think. They tend not to be active or trained listeners and not to build on others' contributions. Other participants should remember that these persons act this way because it fills a need for them. Without trying to make a psychological assess-

ment of the situation, they can help these people express their needs and uniqueness in a way which might better contribute to their development and that of the other participants.

Trainers and discussion leaders often ask, "How can we handle this kind of participant?" as if some psychological trick or a secret procedure should be invoked in order to control his "bad" behavior. There is no need for tricks in a participation-training group. Eventually, as freedom of expression develops, the participants themselves identify and deal with their teamwork problems, of which this is one, in the critique periods that are conducted after each discussion. Meanwhile, patience is required by the trainer and by the other participants. In most cases, a dominator discovers his own limitations as a member of the discussion team. Seldom, indeed, is there necessary a tense, embarrassing situation in which a dominator has to be told that he talks too much. The resolution of the problem usually happens rather naturally.

During critiques and trainer-interruptions, participants are continually reminded of their responsibility to themselves and to each other. When sufficient rapport and acceptance of each other has built up, participants feel free[1] in the critique to talk about their own performance during the discussion. They begin to examine their own participation in the light of discussion teamwork standards. Thus, participants tend over a period of time to recognize their own needs and limitations. This does, however, take time and thoughtful, organized effort.

Unbalanced verbal participation can be graphically illustrated by the trainer or by an observer in either of two ways:

[1]It has been noted by some trainers that groups made up of persons not previously acquainted often achieve this freedom sooner than do persons who know, or think they know, each other.

- He can make a flow chart during the discussion, drawing a line between the originator and recipient of each contribution, and show the chart during the critique.
- He can count the number of times each participant makes a contribution, revealing the number but not the names during the critique.

These devices indicate only quantity of verbal participation. Inevitably they bring up the question of how much verbal participation by one person is too much? There is no absolute answer to this question. What is important is whether participants feel they are dominated or dominating, or are working constructively together, each making his special contribution toward a common goal. Feelings of domination become obstacles to learning and working together.

N. A Good Outline

Some participants are likely to confuse a discussion outline with a teacher's outline. These persons assume that there is some kind of absolute standard by which an outline may be judged "good" or "bad." Teachers usually think of an outline as a teaching device that gives logical order to information that is to be presented to a class. It puts content into an order by which it can be logically explained.

To participants intent on discovering significance on their own terms, the teaching order is not important; the learning order (not logical, but psychological) is important.

These two kinds of outlines differ greatly in form. The teaching outline is often a fairly detailed listing of points, complete with subheads and indentations. The discussion outline is only a skeleton list of related discussion tasks or problems, not of information to be covered. There is no single best way for every group to explore a given topic. Each group must explore it in the way in which participants are most comfortable and most highly motivated.

O. Pressuring Others to Accept the Role of Discussion Leader or Observer

In early sessions, some participants will try to exert pressure on other participants to take the roles of discussion leader, coleader, or observer. The trainer must prevent this from happening. The participants try to get others to take these jobs for several reasons. Here are a few:

▶ He knows more about the topic than others so he should be discussion leader." This reasoning implies that the discussion leader is to be a sort of teacher; or that he will, in his superior wisdom, lead them to the right answers. This he must not do because the group makes the decisions about goals and outline and the discussion leader is neutral.

▶ Some group participants know or assume that a certain member of the group wants to serve in a particular role, and that this member is reluctant to volunteer unless he feels the group wants him.

▶ Some are afraid to volunteer.

Trouble getting someone to take the discussion leader's role, for example, appears in several forms. Someone may ask, "Who has not yet served as discussion leader?" The trainer should immediately interrupt and indicate that this question should not be answered. Occasionally, the problem arises in the first session, when a participant says, "Let's all agree to take a turn serving as discussion leader." This practice, too, should be avoided. Participants must learn to become responsible on their own initiative and in their own time.

P. Participants' Image of the Trainer as Teacher

Most trainers are persons whom participants have known as teachers, leaders, or possessors of special information in some subject area. This is one reason why participants first think of a trainer as a teacher in the traditional sense. Their past educational experiences have reinforced the image of an educational leader as mainly a content expert. Thus, some participants find it difficult to understand why the trainer does not give them answers or information about their subjects. Teachers are traditionally answer-givers, and are usually not instruments to help persons become responsible during and for the learning process.

The trainer is, in a sense, a teacher. He is not less a teacher because he refuses to give his answers to all the questions he is asked. He helps participants work out their own answers. The training group experience is not so much an information-presenting experience as it is an exploring or information-applying experience. It is a particular kind of educational experience and calls for a particular kind of teacher—the kind who assists an assemblage of persons to become an effective learning group.

Q. When the Trainer Is Asked a Question about the Subject or Topic

Difficulty arises when participants direct questions concerning content to the trainer. Particularly, the trainer should avoid giving his opinion when the content questions involve his interpretation of information or his taking a personal stand on one side of an issue. He loses some of his effectiveness as a trainer when he emphasizes his personal views on the content. He should tell the participants how to get information themselves through such available sources as records, films, books, magazines, newspapers, and resource people (subject matter experts). The trainer usually should not fill the roles of both trainer and resource person. An important step in the adult learning program is promoted by having participants do things for themselves.

R. Taking Turns

The procedure which involves asking each person for comments at a particular point in a meeting is not appropriate for a training group. It will force everyone to say something, whether he has anything worthwhile to say or not. Compulsion violates the principle of voluntary participation. The leader is justified, however, in asking direct questions if he has reason to believe that the person wishes to say something, or will not be embarrassed by a direct question.

S. Using Mimeographed Topic, Goal(s), and Outline

Participants tend to accept uncritically and do not feel free to adjust whatever appears in printed form. Mimeographed or typed copies of topic, goals, and outline tend to freeze the structure of the discussion. Making these elements visible on an easel or chalkboard is usually more appropriate because they are seen as provisional.

T. Failure to Conduct a Verbal Critique after Each Discussion

In early sessions, trainers are often tempted to omit the verbal critique after each session. It is a mistake to defer it until participants know each other better. The critique is itself one means of developing freedom of expression. The procedure of openly appraising their discussion teamwork becomes established at the first training session and can more easily be continued thereafter. Trainers who defer initiating critiques or who omit them after a few sessions often do so because:

- ▶ They fear that some embarrassing situation will arise.
- ▶ They know that critiques are often superficial in the early sessions and that they will have to take an active part in leading them.
- ▶ They dislike helping a group do something that participants seem reluctant to do. The trainer feels the need to be liked by the group.
- ▶ The group participants have such a good discussion

that he hesitates to dim their satisfaction by having a critique in which they face their limitations as a group.

▶ They are reluctant to initiate critiques because they misunderstand their role and think that they are supposed to criticize individuals in the group during the critique. This is not the trainer's role. He attacks the problem, not the person.

U. Discussion Topics which Call for a "Yes" or "No" Answer

There are two good reasons why any learning group, including a discussion-training group, should avoid phrasing discussion topics in such a way as this: "Should a person be told that he has an incurable disease?"

In the first place, the learning group meets to experience participation training and to explore and better understand topical subjects, not make group decisions or judgments on them. "Yes" or "no" topics, such as our illustration, call for black-and-white thinking, which hinders the group from adequately exploring the grays—those many problems and questions to which there is no known absolute answer.

Participants should be helped to analyze, weigh, and evaluate problems based on solid evidence. Such an approach usually results in a realistic answer which will not be found in any extreme.

Second, topics like that of our illustration encourage participants to line up on two sides and debate the questions. Debate tends to defeat creative learning. It encourages the self-centered urge to win, often at the cost of sincerity. It also attempts to prove one side wrong and the other right through argument and it stimulates negative feelings which separate learners. Advocates of the debate justify it by saying that participants learn to develop their powers of rationality by engaging in intellectual combat, that they improve their use of reason and their ability to make logical choices. But again we must remember that we do not learn productive participation by logic alone or by defending intellectual positions. Feelings, not logic, play the greater part in the learning role.

The major task is not to produce verbal consistency or to become adept at handling controversy. The art of intellectual self-defense may be important, but the fact is, people are emotional beings, and they learn creatively and productively not by defending themselves from others' attacks, not necessarily by being shown they are logically wrong, but by being helped to examine the problem fully in a nonthreatening atmosphere of acceptance. Then they are better able emotionally to accept and use logic and reason toward the kind of personal change which advances them in the maturation process.

A Weekend[1]

Schedule for Participation Training

This outline of events for a weekend training program can be used for either an away-from-home weekend or for a stay-at-home series of sessions. Mealtimes are listed here as sessions because, especially in an away-from-home conference, eating together can be a significant means of achieving the training goals.

In the same respect, trainees who voluntarily share recreation and other activities between sessions can learn to know each other better and develop conditions that help achieve the training goals.

It is important that participants in these weekend conferences have from six to eight actual discussion sessions—at least 12 contact hours of discussion and critique. The temptation to strip down the program to four sessions has been noted many times in field experience. This temptation must be resisted and a realistic time table established. Effective learning of this kind does not take place on an accelerated basis.

---

[1]It should be recalled that the weekend program is only a good beginning to the complete participation-training program, which program may extend several months.

FRIDAY

Registration:	5:00- 6:00 P.M.	
Session 1 :	6:00- 7:00 P.M.	Dinner together
Session 2 :	7:30- 9:30 P.M.	Orientation (purpose of weekend sessions; conditions of effective group participation) Discussion and critique demonstrations led by trainer Planning next session (deciding on goals, outlines, and volunteer leaders) Dispensing reading materials and assignments

SATURDAY

Session 3 :	7:00- 8:00 A.M.	Breakfast together (optional)
Session 4 :	8:00- 9:30 A.M.	Two 30-minute discussions, each followed by a 15-minute critique, or one discussion of 45 minutes to 1 hour, followed by a critique; trainer-interruptions to point out joint responsibilities and obstacles
	9:30-10:00 A.M.	Break
Session 5 :	10:00-12:00 M.	Same as #4 above
Session 6 :	12:00- 1:30 P.M.	Lunch
Session 7 :	1:30- 3:00 P.M.	One-hour discussion followed by observer's report and critique; periodic trainer interruptions
	3:00- 3:30 P.M.	Break
Session 8 :	3:30- 5:30 P.M.	Same as #7 above
Session 9 :	6:00- 7:00 P.M.	Dinner together
Session 10 :	7:30- 9:00 P.M.	Same as #7 above; or recreation

SUNDAY

Session 11 :	7:00- 9:00 A.M.	Worship service and breakfast together (optional)
Session 12 :	9:00-10:30 A.M.	Same as #7 above (optional)
	10:30-10:45 A.M.	Break
Session 13 :	10:45-12:00 NOON	Same as #7 above
Session 14 :	12:00- 1:30 P.M.	Lunch together

Session 15 : 1:30- 3:30 P.M.   (a) Evaluation of teamwork developed up to this point, led by trainer(s)
(b) Planning follow-up sessions (dates, discussion leaders, observers, and next topic, goals, outline, and resource materials)
(c) Written evaluation of the weekend (optional)

Notes on Weekend Sessions

Session 1: The first meal together should be preceded by some kind of registration procedure in which each participant is given a name tag to wear. If participants know each other, this is not necessary. The name tags should be dispensed with as soon as the participants become acquainted.

Session 2: The first activity in the orientation session might well employ a simple procedure for becoming better acquainted. If participants do not already know each other, a few minutes may be spent profitably by dividing the participants into pairs, letting one of each pair interview the other for three or four minutes, and having each person introduce to the group the person he has interviewed and tell about him for two or three minutes. It is often helpful to have participants reveal at this point what they expect to get out of this weekend. It is useful to know what they think about this experience and what they expect will come of it.

Next, preferably with the help of slides and/or charts, trainer(s) can explain the purpose of the whole participation-training program of which this weekend is but one part. A brief overview describing the nature of the weekend sessions is helpful. Participants wish to know what will happen, what is expected of them, and what they may expect of the trainers.

A brief explanation (with visual aids, if possible) of the roles and conditions of effective participation in learning groups may be given at this point. This explanation should include an introduction to the roles of leader, group participant, and observer.

Next comes a 30- to 45-minute discussion period in which the trainer serves as discussion leader. The topic can come from either the trainer or the group. The trainer-discussion leader can help the group to set or adjust goals rapidly and build or adjust an outline before actually starting the discussion.[2] How the topic, goal(s), and outline are expressed visually is crucial because it helps set a procedural standard for future discussions. (See Chapter 3, "Elements of Structure.") If two trainers are available, the one not serving as discussion leader should make a few brief pertinent trainer-interruptions during this demonstration discussion.

After the discussion, a trainer can lead a critique of the discussion teamwork. The checklist in Appendix B will serve as a guide for helping the participants identify and discuss various aspects of this procedure. Or, if two trainers are available, the one who does not serve as discussion leader can act as observer and give his report as well as initiate the critique. The checklist (Appendix B) can be used to guide a final appraisal analysis after the group has commented upon the observer's report.

Next, the group should determine its topic(s) for the first session on Saturday morning, along with goals and outline, if time is available.[3]

Volunteer coleaders should be secured; also a volunteer observer if the trainer wishes to introduce the observer's role at this early stage. Some trainers prefer to use vol-

---

[2] Often the trainer formulates suggested goals and outline and submits them to the group for modification as soon as he draws a topic out of the group.

[3] An alternate procedure is to let the volunteer leaders develop suggested goals and an outline and let the group adjust them at the beginning of the next session. There are obvious advantages to having a whole group perform this task.

unteer observers for the first time during the Saturday afternoon session from 1:30 to 3:00 P.M.

Finally, the participants should be given some reading material that will help them understand the nature of the training process and the function of responsible participants. The present book is one such resource. Other helpful sources are *Adult Education Procedures,* by Bergevin, Morris, and Smith (Seabury Press, 1963), which deals with group procedures and program planning; *Design for Adult Education in the Church,* by Bergevin and McKinley (Seabury Press, 1961, second printing), which describes how to adapt participation training to an institutional setting; and *Creative Methods for Adult Classes,* by McKinley (Bethany Press, 1960), which describes conditions of group participation.

Sessions 4 and 5: There is often some advantage to conducting two 30-minute discussions rather than one longer discussion, because four volunteers have an opportunity to serve as coleaders in the space of 1½ hours, and eight persons by noon on Saturday. One of the best ways for participants to understand the significance of responsible group participation is to serve in the role of discussion leader.

The short 30-minute discussion periods do not yield the participants much content satisfaction from the subject matter discussed. They do, however, give the group multiple experiences in dealing with four sets of goals and outlines. In addition, in these two 1½-hour sessions four verbal critiques are conducted and the participants become more ready to focus on topics that are personally significant and on topics with which they are able to deal.

Session 7: This discussion period and all subsequent ones should be about one hour in length, or perhaps one hour and ten minutes. The last 20 to 30 minutes in each session is given to the observer's report, the critique, and to setting up the topic, goals, outline, and deciding on the volunteer discussion leaders and observer for the next session.

Session 8: Near the end of this session, before the participants plan their next discussion, some trainers find it useful to help the group define the characteristics of a productive topic. The trainer must not let himself be trapped into suggesting a topic for the group, wording or phrasing a chosen topic for the group, or indicating his preference of several topics suggested by the participants. The participants must solve these problems themselves.

Sessions 12 and 13. These sessions should yield more satisfaction to the participants at the topic level. It would be useful for the trainer to meet with the volunteer observer for each of these sessions before the session begins, to review the observer's duties. Effective observer's reports are good preludes to effective verbal critiques after each discussion. By this time, the trainer should be encouraging the volunteer discussion leaders and the group members to proceed directly into the observer's report and critique at the conclusion of each discussion. In other words, the group should start to become as self-directing as possible—one of the ultimate objectives of this kind of learning. The trainer is needed mainly for occasional trainer-interruptions, as "clean-up" man at the end of the critiques, and for consultation with participants between sessions.

Session 15: This last two-hour session has three tasks. Time allotments can be adjusted as advisable. The first task is that of critically appraising the teamwork that has developed up to this point. This can be a significant hour and a half of learning if enough freedom and understanding have developed. It is led by the trainer and conducted as a discussion. One way to proceed is for the group to identify ways they think they fail as individuals in working as a team. For each limitation they identify, they should be encouraged to discuss its cause, its effect, and ways to overcome it. Time should also be given to identifying new understandings and skills that have been learned—in other words, ways in which they succeeded in working as a learning team, and why.

The second task is to plan for additional meetings. Weekly follow-up meetings have been found more effective than bi-weekly meetings. To follow up a weekend program, additional weekly sessions are usually 1½ to 2 hours in length. Inevitably a few participants will ask whether two or three friends can join the group at the next meeting. Sometimes new participants can join without undue difficulty. In general, it is not good policy to expand the group at this point. But it is possible to start a new group. Some of the inspired participants will assist in this expansion.

The next task might be to get a written appraisal of the weekend from the participants. These unsigned appraisals are valuable to trainers who wish to improve their next weekend conference. Three or four questions such as these will give purpose to the appraisals: (1) What did you like least about this part of the participation-training program? (2) What did you like most about this part of the participation-training program? (3) How could the next program like this be improved?

The final task is to make sure that all the participants who took part in this first phase of the participation-training program know that the program is not completed and that the part just completed is a good start, that everyone knows the exact time and place of the next meeting and that they should support one another to see to it that they all finish the job they started.

A Check List
for Conducting Critiques

Careful consideration of each of the following points will
assist participants in evaluating their progress in their learning efforts:

1. Individual preparation for discussion
2. Interest in topic
3. Clarity of goals
4. Clarity of tasks
5. Progress toward sharing in making decisions on subject matter, procedures, and processes
6. Freedom of discussion
7. Helping others take part
8. Exploring alternative ideas
9. Building upon others' ideas
10. Listening to each other
11. Barriers to communication
12. Asking for clarification
13. Dependence on leader
14. Dependence on trainer
15. Use of recorder
16. Use of resource person
17. Achievement of goals
18. Assuming personal responsibility for program's success

A Glossary of Terms

Acceptance: an uncensuring attitude toward a person's behavior and recognition of his worth as a person without condemning or condoning his actions or expressions.

Change goals: desired results or outcomes expressed in terms of behavior changes among participants.

Coleader: a participant whose primary responsibility is to help the discussion leader to coordinate the discussion; may involve the duties of recorder.

Combination entry: a type of trainer-interruption in which the trainer presents a brief lecture on some educational concept, procedure, role, or process factor that is pertinent.

Consensus: an agreement which is usually the result of concessions made when the majority and the minority views are evaluated and taken into consideration to modify the decision; a tentative working agreement.

Critique: a period of appraisal during which the participants assess the quality of their discussion.

Discussion leader: a participant whose primary responsibility is to help the group participants work together effectively toward achievement of group goals.

Focusing process: the adjusting of topic, goals, and outline to each other in such a way that they are made more explicit, specific, and mutually supporting.

Goal: a desired result or outcome which participants hope to achieve.

Group discussion: a purposeful, cooperative exploration of a topic of mutual interest by six to twenty persons under the guidance of a trained leader.

Group participants: the persons who discuss the topic and for whose benefit the discussion exists; all other participants perform service roles to help the group participants.

Leader: (see discussion leader)

Observation entry: a type of trainer-interruption in which the trainer presents focused observations of the group's process or procedure.

Observer: a participant whose major responsibility is to observe how the group functions as a discussion team and to report his observations when called upon—usually in the critique period.

Outline, discussion: a series of discussion tasks which define the sequence and the nature of the content of the discussion.

Participant: a person who takes part in the training program by assuming one of these roles: trainer, discussion leader, group participant, observer, resource person, co-leader, or recorder. All of these participants working together toward common goals would be considered a *learning team.*

Participation training: in this book, a program designed to help participants learn how to use the processes and procedures of group discussion more effectively.

Points of focus: places in the wording of topics, goals, and outlines where adjustments could make them more specific.

Points of withdrawal: critical points in the developing program at which trainers should withdraw their initial leadership as the other participants become able to assume the responsibility.

Procedure: a systematic series of actions designed to accomplish a task.

Process: the flow of all the intra- and inter-personal factors involved in how persons communicate and learn as opposed to what they communicate and learn (content).

Program: a series of educational meetings, called training sessions, in which participants try to achieve educational goals.

Question entry: a type of trainer-interruption in which the trainer raises a question about the group's process or procedure.

Recorder: a participant whose primary responsibility is to record the development of the discussion on a chalkboard or large chart pad.

Resource person: a person who has had special training and/ or significant experience in the subject that is discussed and who serves the group by furnishing authoritative information when called upon.

Task: a job to be done; an instrumental activity that leads to the achieving of a goal.

Task goal: a task the completion of which is considered one type of outcome yielding feelings of goal achievement.

Teaching interlude: a type of trainer-interruption in which the trainer presents a brief lecture on some educational concept, procedure, role, or process factor that is pertinent.

Topic: a subject to be discussed; a problem stated as a question not answerable by "yes" or "no."

Topic area: a subject within which it is possible to identify several specific topics.

Trainer: the participant who is trained to help all other participants understand and use group processes and procedures more effectively.

Trainer interruption: a term used to describe the action of a trainer when he intervenes in the discussion in order to teach the participants about process and procedure.

Trainer's introduction: a period of from five to fifteen minutes at the start of a training session during which the trainer gives a short lecture; used most often in early sessions.

Index

G

Glossary, 101-104
Goals, definition, 101, 102
  distinguishing from tasks and topics, 45-46
  identification, 37
  not fully understood, 74
  problems and obstacles, 38-39, 80-81
  written record, 79-80, 90
Government groups, 17
Group discussion, definition, 102
Group participant (*see* Participant, group)
Group process, 31 (*see* Process)
Groups, behavioral standards, 64
  composition, 17
  effective operating conditions, 34-35
  recruitment, 19
  size, 16
  stages of development, 68-71

H

Hospital groups, 17

I

Inactive leader, 84-85
Independence, competitive, 69-71
  cooperative, 71
Industrial groups, 17
Informational materials (*see* Resource materials)

L

Leader, discussion, 101
  definition, 101
  description, 25
  dominating, 83-84
  forcing participation, 88
  inactive, 84-85
  responsibilities, 26-27
Leadership (*see* Leader, discussion)
Leadership training, 17
Learners, and teamwork, 60, 71, 98-99
  rate of learning, 18, 19
Length of sessions, 16

Listening, 35
Location of sessions, 16

M

Maturation, 18-19, 92
Meetings, attendance, 16
  initial meeting, 21
  length, 16
  number, 12-15
  place, 16
  shared planning, 22
  time and place, 99
Military groups, 17

O

Observation entry, definition, 102
  use, 55
Observer, definition, 102
  responsibilities, 31
  suggestions for observing, 31-32, 98
Observing, comprehensive, 31
  factors to look for, 31
  selective, 31
Organizational meeting, 21
Orientation session, 95-97
Outline, definition, 102
  function, 39
  importance, 87
  written record, 79-80, 90

P

Participant, group, definition, 102
  dominating, 85-86
  definition, 102
  responsibilities, 29-31
Participants, definition, 102
  duties, 25
  idea of education, 74
  initial concerns, 74
  image of the trainer, 88-89
  newcomer in groups, 99
  perspectives, 71-72
  roles, 23
Participation training, and psychodynamics, 19
  and sociodynamics, 19
  contrasted with leadership training, 17

3458